OVERTURE (

in associ

We are delighted to have the opportunity to work with Overture Publishing on this series of opera guides and to build on the work ENO did over twenty years ago on the Calder Opera Guide Series. As well as reworking and updating existing titles, Overture and ENO have commissioned new titles for the series and all of the guides will be published to coincide with repertoire being staged by the company at the London Coliseum.

In recent years ENO has enjoyed a series of highly successful and critically acclaimed productions of Britten's operas, including Deborah Warner's *Death in Venice*, David McVicar's *Turn of the Screw* and David Alden's *Peter Grimes*. Opening on 19th May 2011 is the latest instalment of this refreshing of the Britten repertoire: Christopher Alden's new production of *A Midsummer Night's Dream*, conducted by Leo Hussain and with a cast led by counter-tenor Iestyn Davies (Oberon), soprano Anna Christy (Tytania) and bass-baritone Sir Willard White (Bottom).

We hope that these guides will prove an invaluable resource now and for years to come, and that by delving deeper into the history of an opera, the poetry of the libretto and the nuances of the score, readers' understanding and appreciation of the opera and the art form in general will be enhanced.

John Berry
Artistic Director, ENO
May 2011

The publisher John Calder began the Opera Guides series under the editorship of the late Nicholas John in association with English National Opera in 1980. It ran until 1994 and eventually included forty-eight titles, covering fifty-eight operas. The books in the series were intended to be companions to the works that make up the core of the operatic repertory. They contained articles, illustrations, musical examples and a complete libretto and singing translation of each opera in the series, as well as bibliographies and discographies.

The aim of the present relaunched series is to make available again the guides already published in a redesigned format with new illustrations, some new articles, updated reference sections and a literal translation of the libretto that will enable the reader to get closer to the meaning of the original. New guides of operas not already covered will be published alongside the redesigned ones from the old series.

Gary Kahn
Series Editor

Sponsors of the Overture Opera Guides

for the 2010/11 Season at ENO

A Midsummer Night's Dream

Benjamin Britten

Overture Opera Guides
Series Editor
Gary Kahn

Editorial Consultant
Philip Reed
Head of Publications, ENO

OVERTURE

OVERTURE OPERA GUIDES
in association with

EN
O

Overture Publishing
an imprint of

ONEWORLD CLASSICS
London House
243-253 Lower Mortlake Road
Richmond
Surrey TW9 2LL
United Kingdom

Printed in United Kingdom by TJ International, Padstow, Cornwall

ISBN: 978-1-84749-544-0

Contents

List of Illustrations

1. Benjamin Britten at a press conference in Amsterdam before the opening of *A Midsummer Night's Dream* at the Holland Festival on 11th July 1960, one month after the premiere in Aldeburgh.

2. Peter Pears and Benjamin Britten in the early 1960s (above).
3. The Red House, Aldeburgh in the early 1960s, where Britten and Pears
lived and worked from 1957 (below).

THE ACTORS' NAMES

THESEUS, Duke of Athens
~~EGEUS, father to Hermia~~

LYSANDER ⎫ in love with Hermia
DEMETRIUS ⎭

~~PHILOSTRATE, Master of the Revels to Theseus~~

N. Lumsd   QUINCE, a carpenter   (*Prologue*)
T. Anthony   SNUG, a joiner   (*Lion*)   — *slow*
O. Brannigan   BOTTOM, a weaver   (*Pyramus*)
H. Cuenod   FLUTE, a bellows-mender   (*Thisby*)   — *high*
David Kelly   SNOUT, a tinker   (*Wall*)   — *old man*
       STARVELING, a tailor   (*Moon*)   — *thin*

HIPPOLYTA, Queen of the Amazons, betrothed to
     Theseus
HERMIA, daughter to Egeus, in love with Lysander *small*
HELENA, in love with Demetrius   *tall*
OBERON, King of the Fairies
TITANIA, Queen of the Fairies
PUCK, or Robin Goodfellow

?   PEASEBLOSSOM ⎫
1   COBWEB   ⎬ fairies
4   MOTH   ⎪
3   MUSTARDSEED ⎭

Orch.
4 2 ? ? ?
2 ! 2 !
! 2 !
2 ! 2

4. Britten's annotated cast list in his Penguin edition of
Shakespeare's *A Midsummer Night's Dream*.

5. The first page of Britten's composition draft for Act One of
A Midsummer Night's Dream.

6. Britten rehearsing the boys playing the Fairies in the Jubilee Hall,
Aldeburgh for the first production, June 1960 (above).

7. The first production, directed by John Cranko and designed by John Piper.
Edward Byles as Snout/Wall, Peter Pears as Flute/Thisby, April Cantelo as
Helena and Thomas Hemsley as Demetrius (below).

8. Russell Oberlin, who played Oberon, and John Gielgud, who directed the first London production, at the Royal Opera House in February 1961. The designer, as at Aldeburgh, was John Piper (above).

9. Elizabeth Vaughan as Tytania and Josephine Veasey as the mezzo-soprano Oberon in the revival of the Royal Opera House production in 1966 (below).

10. Günther Rennert's production, designed by Helmut Jürgens, at the Hamburg Staatsoper in February 1961 (above).
11. Luigi Squarzina's production, designed by Fabrizio Clerici, at La Scala, Milan in April 1961 (below).

12. Rudolf Asmus as Bottom and Ella Lee as Tytania in the production
directed by Walter Felsenstein and designed by Rudolf Heinrich at
the Komische Oper, Berlin in July 1961 (above).
13. Basil Coleman's production, designed by Harry Horner, at the San Francisco
Opera Company in October 1961. Geraint Evans (far left) as Bottom (below).

14. The rustics, with Puck behind them, in the production directed by Johan Van der Bracht and designed by Lou de Vel at the Royal Flemish Opera, Antwerp in 1962 (above).
15. The production directed and designed by Jean-Pierre Ponnelle at the Strasbourg Festival in 1966 (below).

16. Peter Hall's production, designed by John Bury, at the Glyndebourne Festival. Elizabeth Gale as the sleeping Tytania in 1984. The production was seen at the festival for five seasons between 1981 and 2006.

17. Danielle Borst as Helena and François Le Roux as Demetrius arriving in the wood in the production directed by Moshe Leiser and Patrice Caurier and designed by Jacques Rapp and Moshe Leiser at the Opéra de Lyon in 1983 (above).
18. Mark Rylance as Puck and James Bowman as Oberon in the production directed by Christopher Renshaw and designed by Robin Don at the Royal Opera House in 1986 (below).

19. The lovers suspended in their beds, with James Bowman (Oberon) and Emil Wolk (Puck) below, in the production directed by Robert Carsen and designed by Michael Levine at the Aix-en-Provence Festival in 1991. It was first seen at ENO in 1995 (above).

20. Lorina Gore as Tytania and Joshua Tate as the Indian Boy in Baz Luhrmann's production, designed by Catherine Martin and Bill Barran, at Opera Australia in 1993. It came to the Edinburgh Festival in 1994 (below).

21. Act Three of Tim Albery's production, designed by Antony McDonald, at the Metropolitan Opera in 1996 (above).

22. Puck (David Greeves) overlooking the sleeping Tytania (Laura Claycomb) and Fairies in David McVicar's production, designed by Rae Smith, at La Monnaie, Brussels in 2004 (below).

Night's Caressing Grip:
The Evolution of the *Dream*

Andrew Plant

> *A strong moon pitches their shadows forward:*
> *Sounds of their footsteps break against the woody masses*
> *But the tide in the tall trees is taciturn, another life.*
>
> W.H. Auden and Christopher Isherwood,
> from *The Dog beneath the Skin* (1935)

Undertones and visions of the half-light run like a shimmering thread through Britten's output. Most of his operas contain *Nachtmusik* of supreme beauty but the tally of independent night scenes is as remarkable as the scrutiny brought to bear on each facet of such imagery; indeed, the allure of the subconscious world appears to strengthen and its power to deepen on each ensuing manifestation. The juvenile frivolity of 'The Ride-by-Nights' that is the first of Britten's Three Two-part Songs of 1932 (one of his very earliest published works – though not, it should be emphasized, one of his earliest works per se), 'Night' from *Holiday Diary*, 'Lullaby' from the Suite op. 6, Auden's 'Nocturne' in *On this Island*, the similarly titled movements in Diversions, *Matinées Musicales* and the Harp Suite, the *Night Piece*, the Goethe setting 'Um Mitternacht', the *Nocturnal after John Dowland*: these are only the most obvious instances of the composer's lifelong absorption. Then, of course, there is the subject matter of the 1947 cycle *A Charm of Lullabies*, for which Britten also wrote two further settings that were later discarded; and the two orchestral cycles: *Serenade* of 1943 (itself containing yet another 'Nocturne', this time Tennyson's) and particularly the eponymous *Nocturne* itself, completed only two years before *A Midsummer Night's Dream*.

From the outset, the *Dream* was linked to Britten's vision for the future of the Aldeburgh Festival. Plans for a purpose-built theatre had been under occasional discussion since 1948, but now that a suitable site in the town centre had been identified, he hoped for a flexible new resource in time for the thirteenth Festival in 1960. When it became clear that financial constraints still made the project unfeasible, Britten's thoughts turned instead to the refurbishment of the existing Jubilee Hall, where many Festival performances had already been held. On 22nd July 1959, soon after the decision was made to write an opera to celebrate the hall's reopening, the composer visited John and Myfanwy Piper. This was no mere courtesy call but an essential early step in the creative process, which two days later he reported to Peter Pears, who was fulfilling engagements in Germany:

> They were thrilled at the idea of Midsummer Night's Dream & we discussed it endlessly. I'm just sending off to Myfanwy our projected scheme for it; she has some good ideas about it. John was most useful and full of suggestions about the look of it, but we couldn't really settle on the producer. Basil Coleman & Johnny Cranko the first choices (latter slight favourite)…

Letter to Peter Pears, 24th July 1959[1]

Britten can hardly have been short of possible subjects but had also been considering Shakespeare for some years. Despite his later rather glib explanation that the libretto was ready to hand, the text was by no means suitable as it stood, and to fashion it for the purpose was a great labour, most of which Britten credited to Pears. Both men possessed copies of the Penguin text, in which Britten noted character traits and Pears planned the scenario and pacing. The tenor also

1   Philip Reed and Mervyn Cooke (eds), *Letters from a Life: The Selected Letters of Benjamin Britten 1913–1976*, vol. 5 (Woodbridge: The Boydell Press, 2010), p. 161.

wrote a draft cast list inside the back cover, indicating that he was to undertake the role of Starveling, doubling as Moonshine in the play. Britten had wished him to play Lysander but many of Pears's external concert commitments were already confirmed, preventing his assumption of such a major character. When Starveling was developed into a baritone role, Pears undertook the part of Flute, replacing Britten's original choice of the Swiss tenor, Hugues Cuénod, who was unavailable. The composer then approached William McAlpine as a substitute Lysander, but the part was eventually created by George Maran. After considerable industry, a typewritten transcription of the new libretto was prepared from Pears's copy.

Having ensured the availability of essential colleagues, Britten's next most pressing task was to reschedule current plans, notably the development of what would become *Curlew River*, the first of the three Church Parables. The composer wrote apologetically to his librettist William Plomer in August to explain that the subject was unsuitable for a festive opening in such a venue. In a later letter, he added:

> If I could sometime send you the cutting & cooking of Shakespeare I've been indulging in, with Peter's help, these last weeks, I'd love to, for a comment or two if you have them – a fascinating problem, only heart-breaking to have to leave out so much wonderful stuff – the comfort being that, if one didn't, it would play as long as the 'Ring'.

Letter to William Plomer, 24th August 1959[2]

A long-standing invitation from the Earl of Harewood to write a Sea Symphony for the Leeds Festival had also to be postponed, a work that was fated to progress no further than the selection of possible texts in the composer's final years. Britten then commenced securing his *Dream* cast, although since he nearly always wrote with specific voices in mind, it is likely that much of their music had already been conceived. Owen Brannigan accepted the role of Bottom with grateful deference, and on 18th August 1959 the composer approached Alfred Deller:

---

2   Ibid., p. 171.

I wonder how you would react to the idea of playing Oberon in this? It is for a big cast, and each group of people has to be carefully calculated vocally. I see you and hear your voice very clearly in this part, but before I start to write it I should love to know your reactions...

Letter to Alfred Deller, 18th August 1959[3]

Deller, though equally delighted, confessed that it took him two days to recover from the shock of the invitation, and was anxious that the composer should be aware of his comfortable vocal range of an eleventh. His principal aria, 'I know a bank where the wild thyme blows', would pay homage not only to Purcell but also to Deller's own outstanding abilities in the performance of Baroque music.

At the beginning of October, Britten and Pears drove to Venice with the artist Mary Potter for a two-week holiday, where the composition draft was begun:

The place is bewilderingly lovely in this summer weather, & I'm now developing a nice routine of work all morning, picnic lunch, in some quiet square usually if possible containing a masterpiece, wandering around churches & galleries in the afternoon, more work in the early evening & experimenting with out-of-the-way restaurants in the evenings! The opera is just beginning to stir, but too young yet to know if it's going to be an obedient or intractable child, interesting or boring...

Letter to the Earl of Harewood, 8th October 1959[4]

Further vital personnel were contacted on their return, including Jennifer Vyvyan in the role of Titania (the revised spelling of Tytania was not adopted until early the following year). 'I can hear you in what I've written so far,' Britten assured her. Thomas Hemsley was to sing Demetrius, while the casting of boys as the fairy chorus had been decided by November, as Britten wrote to the soprano Olive Dyer to explain that his decision had been prompted by Shakespeare's title of

3   Ibid., p. 173.
4   Ibid., pp. 186 and 188.

'mounseer' for them. The part of Puck was designed for a boy acrobat and created by the son of Léonide Massine, the great Russian dancer, choreographer of the Ballets Russes and heir to Nijinsky's roles.

Britten worked at phenomenal speed and began Act Two on 9th December, while his amanuensis, Imogen Holst, began producing the vocal score of Act One. Only two minor characters had been excised – those of Egeus (Hermia's father) and Philostrate (Master of the Revels to Theseus) – but most of the scenario had already been distilled into one overarching night, and the composer began to fear that the structure was unstable; as Mervyn Cooke has pointed out, the implication is that both lovers' scenes occur simultaneously. Britten therefore requested a draft Prologue from Myfanwy Piper (author of the libretto for *The Turn of the Screw* in 1954), the evident purpose being to clarify Lysander's reference to 'the sharp Athenian law', for which the explanation had disappeared in the abridgement. Piper borrowed words from the very opening of the play and from a later speech by Theseus, fashioning them into proclamations for two heralds and thereby creating a dramatic moment not unlike that given to the Spirit of the Masque in *Gloriana*. A four-bar sketch survives for the scene but at some point it was abandoned, presumably after further perseverance had determined that the necessary information could be condensed into a single brief aside, 'compelling thee to marry with Demetrius'. This phrase, set to a rapid monotone to distinguish it from the rest of the text, is the only addition to Shakespeare in the entire opera, although a number of minor adaptations were made to accommodate the new time frame, such as Theseus's 'Four happy days bring in another moon', which had necessarily to become 'this happy day brings in another moon'. Most of the other lines used by Piper were restored to Theseus and Hippolyta, although the new scenario placed them in Act Three.

Act Two took barely five weeks to complete and was finished by 14th January, but the relentless pressure of such an astonishing work rate was exacting its toll on the composer. In February, when Holst suddenly required an operation for an ovarian cyst, the race against time was intensified. Martin Penny was summoned to complete the vocal score of Act Three, with some later temporary assistance from Viola Tunnard, even though the full score was still unfinished by the end of March. As the final scenes hurtled to completion, Britten conveyed the news to Pears, who was singing the part of Evangelist in Bach's *St Matthew Passion* at the Concertgebouw, Amsterdam:

> Work's going quite well – I should be finished in a day or two, I hope & pray it's not too bad.
>   John's sent photos of the sets which look <u>ravishing</u>. Full of leaves, & twigs, & branches – a real deep thick wood…
>
> *Undated letter to Peter Pears [before 10th April 1960]*[5]

As estimated, Britten completed the full score on 15th April, less than two months before the premiere, although he still found time to describe its traumatic gestation to Elizabeth Mayer:

> I have had a real wrestle with the angel to get the Midsummer Night's Dream finished (which it should be this week). I have been fighting illness too – the arm which made me cancel all concerts before Xmas, finally made me give up again after a few efforts here & in Holland. It is now diagnosed as gout (– me, who can't stand port!), & I am in the midst of a rather distressing cure – with pills & their antidotes which make one feel pretty desperate […] But you can imagine that working has been difficult, especially a piece which needs so much vitality… Now I must go back to the last scene…
>
> *Letter to Elizabeth Mayer, 11th April 1960*[6]

The other principal figure in these preparations was John Piper, who had provided designs for the premieres of all Britten's operas except *Paul Bunyan*, *The Little Sweep* and *Noye's Fludde*. Britten always wished to know how a proposed stage work would appear before he began writing and it is likely that the artist would have been requested to commence work on Dream as soon as possible. Piper later explained his methods:

---

5   Ibid., p. 215.

6   Ibid., p. 219 and 220.

I thought that in most productions I had seen of the play the scenery was preponderantly green, though it was Midsummer *night*. I had been looking at a lot of Chinese and Japanese brush and wash drawings while hearing Britten's music in early stages on the piano, all of which seemed to me to suggest (as do summer nights) shades of diluted Chinese ink, with sometimes additions of Chinese white, making tones of silver grey. I still find that these, for me, marry reasonably well with this particular music.[7]

When the opera was revived at Covent Garden in 1974, Piper supervised the refurbishment and repainting of his designs, but most were later scrapped, and at the time of writing, only the large backcloth of the waterfall survives.

On 5th June 1960, the *Observer* printed an article entitled 'A New Britten Opera', in which Britten discussed the production of the work, stating that the entire opera, including the libretto, was completed in seven months. 'This is not up to the speed of Mozart or Verdi,' the composer conceded, 'but these days, when the line of musical language is broken, it is much rarer. It is the fastest of any big opera I have written, though I wrote *Let's Make an Opera* in a fortnight.' (Comparisons with Mozart and Verdi notwithstanding, Britten's self-deprecation certainly does not acknowledge that although the *Dream* was his first full-scale opera for five years, he had written six operas in the ten years before that, as well as the recent and substantial three-act ballet, *The Prince of the Pagodas*.) While the pruning of the text was largely dictated by musical considerations, he also admitted:

Peter Pears and I had endless trouble with the references and the proportions of the play [...] I do not feel in the least guilty at having cut the play in half. The original Shakespeare will survive. Nor did I find it daunting to be tackling a masterpiece which already has a strong verbal music of its own. Its music and the music I have written for it are at two quite different levels. I haven't tried to put

7 John Piper, 'Designing for Britten' in David Herbert (ed.), *The Operas of Benjamin Britten* (London: Hamish Hamilton, 1979), p. 7.

across any particular idea of the play that I could equally well express in words, but although one doesn't intend to make any special interpretation, one cannot avoid it.

'A New Britten Opera', Observer, 5th June 1960[8]

These remarks, together with the commonly voiced but debatable assertion that words were not Britten's *métier*, have served to obscure the subtlety with which the co-librettists effected major dramatic changes. It is now possible to see how the opera sits squarely within the lineage of Britten's works that explore unconventional relationships. Shakespeare's play supposedly takes place in Greece but this has no bearing whatever on the plot: it is merely a fabulously mysterious location in which to set an Elizabethan drama. Britten's *Dream* is likewise firmly of Albion, not Athens, but its enchantment contains irresistible exotic undercurrents that first carry the action a considerable distance from the romantic comedy of Weber or Mendelssohn and then turn conformism upside down.

The *Nocturne* contains a hauntingly delicate setting from Coleridge's fragmentary project, 'The Wanderings of Cain':

A lovely Boy was plucking fruits
By moonlight, in a wilderness [...]
Has he no friend, no loving mother near?

Coleridge himself began a translation of Christoph Martin Wieland's Oberon, after which Weber's last opera was modelled; but in returning to the original Shakespeare, Britten and Pears ensured that the catalyst for the *Dream* was not a debate about inconstancy (as in Weber's work) or a celebration of Oberon's birthday (as in Purcell's *The Fairy Queen*) but the fate of a similarly orphaned 'beauteous Boy beguil'd'. Oberon's purpose for the boy is unclear but his already existing relationship with Puck is, as Philip Brett has pointed out, the dominant relationship in the opera. Moreover, the rearrangement of the libretto ensures that the dominion of the supernatural no longer encroaches on the realm of humanity, but precisely the

---

8   The article is reprinted in full on pp. 55–58 [Ed.].

other way about. As with the *Nocturne*, in which the central pre-occupation is with night, sleep and dreams, the opera opens in 'The Wood – deepening twilight' and remains there through the increased darkness of Act Two, until the morning lark of Act Three. The status quo is thus established not as the bright environment of the ducal court but as the shadowy-forested fairy kingdom, the irregular and contradictory becoming the inescapable touchstone of normality. The audience as well as the lovers are captured with as much ease and with as little comprehension as was Thomas the Rhymer, laughing at the foibles of their counterparts, and so blinded by Oberon's spell they are unable to see the trees for the wood. The appearance of Theseus and his retinue is delayed until Act Three, when many of their concerns seem dim and unimportant in the bright light of day. Unlike the enticements of Britten's *Serenade*, the baying of the Duke's hunting horns do not lure us into enchanted twilight, they wake us from it. Clearly, not all such subversion was intended, including a Freudian error overlooked until 1999, when Mervyn Cooke observed that the rearrangement of Shakespeare's text had resulted in the pairs of lovers retiring to bed unmarried. While it may therefore be regretted that the composer declined to set such gems as Oberon's elegiac lines, 'Even till the eastern gate, all fiery-red / Opening on Neptune with fair blessed beams / Turns into yellow gold his salt green streams', perhaps the retention of Puck's triumphant cry, 'Lord, what fools these mortals be!' was never in doubt.

Despite Britten's meteoric rate of progress, only a few revisions were made, notably a new version of the Lion's solo that was first heard at the London performances of 1961. Act Three also contains an optional cut that was omitted at the premiere and not included in Britten's recording: it is a significant exchange between the lovers that emphasizes the transience of their own world:

LYSANDER
    Are you sure that we are awake?
    It seems to me
    That we yet sleep, we dream.

HERMIA
   Methinks I see these things with pointed eye
   When everything seems double.

DEMETRIUS
   These things seem small and undistinguishable
   Like far-off mountains turned into clouds.

If this cut is made, it throws a quite different light on the final out-come, for the lovers then assert instead, 'We are awake,' so empha-sizing that their finding of each other 'like a jewel' is no illusion but firm reality. The alternative reading delays their acknowledgement of wakefulness until *after* the reconciliations, when their joint statement is altogether more gentle and uncertain; and as they wander out of sight, it is not clear whether they were already simply recounting their dreams. As after a heavy sleep, when matters of seemingly vital importance appear less pressing, so the arrangements for the impending nuptials are quickly passed over in order that the main focus of the party may become the rustics' play. Already an absurdly overblown charade, this fond pageant of lions, moonshine and trou-bled relationships is fiercely caricatured further through Britten's filter of Schoenbergian parody and a hilariously distorted burlesque of nineteenth-century *bel canto*. The final return of the fairies to consecrate the house is therefore perceived not as an uncanny occur-rence but a blessed resumption of the familiar, of lasting associations and peace that endures.

Britten dedicated the work to Stephen Reiss, general manager of the Festival, who oversaw the conversion of the Jubilee Hall and would later supervise the conversion of Snape Maltings. The refurbishment included a larger auditorium, a well-equipped stage, new dressing rooms and the provision of a reasonably generous orchestra pit holding about forty players, but the premiere of what the composer described as a 'slightly large chamber [opera]' strained the parochial resource to the limit, with Britten forced to reduce the number of strings to twelve. At the eleventh hour, owing to the illness of the second harpist, it was necessary to combine the two harp parts so that they could be played (by Osian Ellis) on one instrument, although space was at such a premium that this was probably a blessing in disguise. Public acclaim for the work was nonetheless considerable, although there were some reservations concerning Deller's stagecraft and Cranko's direction. The internal drama of 'Pyramus and Thisby'[9] received particular praise, especially Pears's performance as Flute/Thisby and his none-too-subtle evocation of Joan Sutherland as Lucia di Lammermoor. Following four performances at Aldeburgh, the work received highly successful stagings in ten international opera houses within a year, including Hamburg and San Francisco; in fact, plans for such had been developing when barely a note of the score had been written. The Aldeburgh production was seen at the Holland Festival in July 1960 with some significant cast changes, although the tour was unfortunately hampered by bad weather and illness.

Deller invariably sang Oberon with immense poise and beauty but the role was his operatic debut and it was abundantly clear that his acting capabilities did not match his vocal achievements. Sadly, the circumstances could scarcely have been less favourable to him. A large figure swathed in a capacious black robe ('half mandarin and half Prospero', as Desmond Shawe-Taylor remarked), he was disconcerted by John Cranko's direction and uncomfortable on the tiny stage, which was crowded with scenery and twenty-four other cast members. Desperately aware of the published criticism, he wrote to Britten offering to withdraw, but the composer responded by return: 'I am <u>sure</u> the idea of your doing Oberon was a good one & the realisation by you of my idea is really wonderful.' When the opera moved to Covent Garden on 2nd February the following year for its first London performance, Britten was particularly incensed at the displacement of Deller by the American counter-tenor Russell Oberlin, who later gave the first US performance in October. The London production was directed by John Gielgud, with choreography by Pirmin Trecu (creator of the role of The Fool in *The Prince of the Pagodas* in 1957), and conducted with understanding by Georg Solti, later touring to Edinburgh and Leeds. Britten was too ill to attend the opening night in London or many of the rehearsals, although

---

9   Britten and Pears adopted this spelling of the name of Shakespeare's Thisbe
    in their libretto [Ed.].

few of the new cast were to his liking: he nearly always regarded his own productions as definitive.

The optimistic critic of *The Times* had assured readers that 'A counter-tenor Oberon is no obstacle nowadays', but Deller had so few vocal rivals that casting problems dogged the work for some years. Britten agreed in principle to a contralto Oberon but an uncorroborated rumour that he was considering rewriting the part for a high tenor such as Pears only reflected the evident problems faced by international directors. Much to Britten's chagrin, the German premiere at the Hamburg Staatsoper on 21st February 1961 (which the Intendant Rolf Liebermann had requested earnestly the previous October), employed not only a tenor Oberon but a girl Puck and a female chorus; it was ironic that this staging apparently prompted the award of the biennial Hanseatic Goethe Prize to the composer. The Komische Oper, directed by Walter Felsenstein, allotted Oberon to a bass (William Ray) in a production seen twice by Shostakovich. At Strasbourg in 1965, the role was undertaken by a tenor (Michel Sénéchal) and at the Russian premiere on 28th October that year, Oberon was sung by the mezzo Elena Obraztsova, shortly after her debut at the Bolshoi. Grayston Burgess sang the part at Covent Garden for several seasons in the early 1960s, but although he had already appeared at the small theatre in Schwetzingen, it was felt that he too lacked the necessary projection for a larger house, an accusation that had been levelled at Deller even in the Jubilee Hall. After Josephine Veasey was cast for the 1966 revival, the opera was dropped by Covent Garden until 1974. Britten recorded the *Dream* for Decca in 1966, reinstating Deller, although a new Oberon was required for a proposed EOG production to be designed by Emanuele Luzzati the following year. After encouragement from George Malcolm, the young James Bowman presented himself for audition, and the rest is history. Bowman was a sensation in the first Britten opera to be mounted at the new Snape Maltings, and immediately made the role his own. He took part in nine further productions during his career, with appearances for Scottish Opera, Covent Garden (two revivals of the original, and one directed by Christopher Renshaw and designed by Robin Don), Sadler's Wells, Welsh National Opera, Opéra

National du Rhin, Australian Opera and Aix-en-Provence. Perhaps the most memorable of Bowman's productions was Peter Hall's scintillating version for Glyndebourne in 1981, which Pears termed definitive and lamented that the composer could not share. Britten had wished Hall to direct the London premiere at Covent Garden in 1961, but prior commitments prevented it. Long before Bowman sang his last Oberon in a concert performance at the Barbican in 1993, a new generation of singers, led by Michael Chance, had enshrined the role within the repertory and encouraged other composers to write for the voice.

Thanks to this advocacy, the opera quickly became established internationally as one of the great settings of Shakespeare and it remains one of Britten's best-loved works. Yet, for a genius who confessed, 'Night and silence, these are two of the things I cherish most', such an achievement and its precedents should hardly surprise us. In fact, it is quite possible to discern much of the literary world of *Dream* in Auden's consoling nocturnal benediction from *The Dog Beneath the Skin*, which Britten set in 1937, as part of *On this Island*. Over twenty years before the first Puck invited our applause to the brilliant accompaniment of a high trumpet, Britten and Auden had already rocked the ground whereon these sleepers be.

> Now through night's caressing grip
> Earth and all her oceans slip [...]
> Now the ragged vagrants creep
> Into crooked holes to sleep:
> Just and unjust, worst and best,
> Change their places as they rest:
> Awkward lovers lie in fields
> Where disdainful beauty yields [...]
> May sleep's healing power extend
> Through these hours to our friend [...]
> Calmly till the morning break
> Let him lie, then gently wake.

W.H. Auden, from Nocturne

A Midsummer Night's *Dream*: The Music

Philip Reed

The worlds of sleep, dreams (and nightmares), of the unconscious, were of powerful significance to Britten's artistic life and fed into much of his creative work. His output is littered with night-inspired compositions, from instrumental nocturnes such as can be found in the early piano suite *Holiday Diary* (1934), through to the magnificent solo guitar piece, *Nocturnal after John Dowland* (1963), with its explanatory subtitle, 'Reflections on "Come, heavy Sleep"'. Virtually every one of Britten's operas prior to *A Midsummer Night's Dream* includes significant, often hauntingly beautiful and, occasionally, disturbing night music. Think of the nocturnal sounds of the primeval North American forest in *Paul Bunyan* (1941); the 'Moonlight' interlude from *Peter Grimes* (1945); Sid and Nancy's twilight courting in *Albert Herring* (1947); the depiction of cool moonlight (piccolo in its lowest register) in *Billy Budd* (1951) on the eve of the condemned sailor's execution; the garden scene in the second act of *Gloriana* (1953); and the deeply sinister yet, for Miles and Flora, alluring bumps in the night in *The Turn of the Screw* (1954).

Further aspects of the world of sleep and dreams are explored by Britten in his song-cycles with piano and with orchestra. *A Charm of Lullabies* (1947) is a song-cycle of invitations to go to sleep; and in his Pushkin cycle, *The Poet's Echo* (1965), there is even a song devoted to insomnia. The two central works concerned with this preoccupation of Britten's are the celebrated *Serenade* for tenor, horn and strings (1943), which ends with a setting of Keats's invocation to sleep, and the later dreamscape, the orchestral song-cycle, *Nocturne*

(1958), which in effect picks up where the *Serenade* ended.[1] These two orchestral song-cycles, both of which use an anthology of English verse selected and shaped by the composer, are core-curricular in an appreciation of Britten's response to nocturnal imagery, and both cycles look forward to *A Midsummer Night's Dream*, Britten's most concentrated and elaborate musico-dramatic response to the world beyond daily reality.

Britten's *Nocturne* culminates in a setting of Shakespeare's paradoxical *Sonnet 43*, 'When most I wink, then do mine eyes best see'. This turned out to be the composer's first setting of Shakespeare since childhood, a somewhat remarkable fact given Britten's fearlessness in the face of most well-known English poetry (Donne or Hardy, for example). But the Shakespeare sonnet is clearly significant when considered in relation to *A Midsummer Night's Dream*, both within the chronological context – *Nocturne* was written a year prior to the planning of the opera – as well as in terms of their shared subject-matter. Britten's *Observer* article – a rare instance of his writing at length about one of his major works – describes the hurried circumstances of his alighting on Shakespeare's *Dream* for an opera for the Aldeburgh Festival;[2] it is surely likely that his 1958 setting of

1   This is true in a literal musical sense: the principal motif of a rejected song from the earlier cycle, a setting of Tennyson's 'Now sleeps the crimson petal', is identical to that of the 'breathing' ritornello of the *Nocturne*, announced at the cycle's opening. Britten gave the manuscript draft of 'Now sleeps the crimson petal' to a friend in 1943 and the setting did not re-emerge until 1987. It says much for the workings of Britten's subconscious that he hit upon the identical motif across a gap of fifteen years. See Donald Mitchell, '"Now sleeps the crimson petal": Britten's Other *Serenade*', in Mitchell, *Cradles of the New: Writings on Music 1951–1991*, selected by Christopher Palmer and edited by Mervyn Cooke (London: Faber and Faber, 1995), pp. 345–51 and plate 30.

2   See full article on pp. 55–58. In a BBC radio interview with Lord Harewood, broadcast in the series 'People Today' on 23 June 1960, Britten gave a similar account of the origins of *A Midsummer Night's Dream*, but admitted 'I had incidentally thought a few years ago of doing this same piece [i.e. Shakespeare's *Dream*] as an opera'. See Paul Kildea (ed.), *Britten on Music* (Oxford: Oxford University Press, 2003), p. 183.

Sonnet 43 led Britten back towards Shakespeare when searching for a suitable pre-existing text for a new opera to launch the refurbished Jubilee Hall in 1960.

As Andrew Plant has described, the episodic nature of Shakespeare's original made Britten's and Peter Pears's task of compression and reorganization easier than it might have been with a more organically developed dramatic structure, and they were ever alert to the possibilities within the play for musical structures. Certainly, the clarity of the structural arch of each the opera's three acts is one of the work's strengths, as is Britten's achievement in balancing the hierarchy of the three principal character-sets in the opera, which are themselves underpinned by an association with particular instrumental sonorities.

The supernatural world of the fairies – Oberon, Tytania and the chorus of boys (from which Tytania's four attendants, Cobweb, Peaseblossom, Mustardseed and Moth, are drawn) – is characterized by high-pitched voices: counter-tenor, coloratura soprano and boy trebles. Even in the concert hall, the sonority of the counter-tenor voice was not as common in 1960 as it is today, and fifty years ago was virtually unheard in the opera house. In casting Oberon as a counter-tenor Britten turned convention on its head, alighting upon the ideal vocal sound, at once strange yet alluring, to suggest the supernatural. Although it was originally written for the rather 'pure' voice of Alfred Deller,[3] an artist with whom Britten and Pears had worked in the concert hall since the 1940s (see Britten's comments in his *Observer* article, p. 58), Britten was later very much taken by James Bowman's interpretation of the role (he first sang Oberon in the late 1960s): he possessed a

---

3   Deller expressed to Britten reservations about his suitability as Oberon: see Philip Reed and Mervyn Cooke (eds.), *Letters from a Life: The Selected Letters of Benjamin Britten 1913–1976*, vol. 5 (Woodbridge: The Boydell Press, 2010), pp. 228–29. Some reviews of the *Dream*'s premiere expressed the view that the role of Oberon should be rewritten for the tenor voice, and Britten was dismayed to learn that in 1961 the Hamburg Staatsoper production, the first new one outside the UK, had indeed cast Oberon as a tenor (see Reed and Cooke, p. 364).

rather more expressive voice than Deller and was certainly a more confident actor.

The choice of the seraphic counter-tenor voice sent Britten back to his beloved Purcell, whose music (including the semi-opera *The Fairy Queen*, itself based on Shakespeare's *A Midsummer Night's Dream*) he had loved since the early 1940s when he first began making realizations for his recitals with Pears. (Deller was himself a leading Purcellian and had been closely involved in the revival of Purcell's music in the 1940s and 1950s.) Britten modelled Oberon's Act One aria 'I know a bank' [13][4] on Purcell's elaborate vocal manner; here allusions to Purcell's song 'Sweeter than roses', which Britten had once arranged for Pears, can be heard. Other Purcellian echoes in *A Midsummer Night's Dream* include the slow march that heralds Oberon and Tytania's entrance in Act One [6, 7] and the Scotch-snap rhythm of the two-bar ground in the closing fairy ensemble of Act Three [80].

Oberon's queen, Tytania, is also a high voice, designated by the composer as a coloratura soprano, i.e. a light soprano with a flexible instrument capable of florid passage-work. Britten's use of decorative vocal lines for Tytania [22, 33] suggests a further affinity with the music of Purcell. Unlike Oberon's counter-tenor, Britten's choice of the soprano tessitura for Tytania lies closer to operatic convention (sopranos are usually the heroines in opera); this is appropriate, for her character has more specific interaction with the natural world than any of the other fairies and in falling in love with Bottom, she crosses into the sphere of the human characters (albeit one with an ass's head) more than the other supernatural beings.

For his chorus of fairies Britten characteristically employs the robust, at times even aggressive sound of boys' voices. In his *Observer* article he admitted to responding to a 'kind of sharpness in Shakespeare's Fairies' who, as Tytania's guards, have 'in places, martial music': perfect examples of this are Britten's settings of 'You spotted snakes with double tongue' towards the end of Act One [23] and 'Now the hungry lion roars' at the end of Act Three [79]. There is nothing soft-centred or lightweight about their music and

---

4   Numbers in square brackets refer to the Thematic Guide on pp. 59–86 [Ed.].

its idiomatic character clearly derives from Britten's long experience of writing for children, especially boys. Britten further justified his decision to cast the fairies as boys from an explicit suggestion in the play where they are 'rather specifically named by Shakespeare "mounseer" [i.e. monsieur]'.[5]

Puck, the spirit who flits between the mortal and immortal realms causing havoc, is described by Britten as an 'absolutely amoral and yet innocent' figure. Conceived by the composer for an adolescent actor-acrobat, he speaks his lines rather than singing them [20], though Britten gives him a very particular musical 'voice' by associating him throughout with an agile motif on the D trumpet [5].

Britten's rustics, Bottom and his companions, lie at the opposite end of the vocal spectrum from the stratospheric sonorities of the fairy world. They balance the vocal hierarchy with their ensemble of low male voices – two tenors, baritone, bass-baritone and two basses – thereby making a clear distinction between themselves and Oberon et al. Britten follows operatic convention in his casting of these comic characters, as he does in his vocally balanced quartet of lovers – soprano (Helena), mezzo-soprano (Hermia), tenor (Lysander), baritone (Demetrius) – with Theseus and Hippolyta, who only appear in Act Three, supplying the missing voice types of bass and contralto. The vocal balance of the quartet of lovers is at odds with an absence of psychological equanimity for most of the opera, and they nearly always sing in even notes, syllable to syllable.

Britten's orchestral palette in *A Midsummer Night's Dream* is used very broadly to reinforce and evoke the three distinct strata of characters. Puck's virtuoso trumpet (often supported by a tabor) has already been mentioned; the lovers' quartet is usually accompanied by a conventional combination of strings and wind [9, 10, 11 and

---

5   Letter from Britten to Olive Dyer, 19th November 1959: see Reed and Cooke, op. cit, p. 172. Britten had been angered to discover that the 1961 Hamburg Staatsoper production had employed a chorus of girl fairies as well as a 'thigh-slapping, toothy-grinned, tom-boy she-Puck' ('Gains and Losses in Britten's *Dream*', *The Times* (22nd February 1961)).

21], while Bottom and his tradesmen companions are characterized by low-pitched instruments (notably trombone for Bottom himself: [15], [16]) or higher instruments playing in their lower registers (e.g. clarinets). To complement the high tessitura of the supernatural characters, Britten reserves specific high-pitched instruments, notably a brace of harps, a harpsichord (a further homage to Purcell), celesta and a small assortment of tuned and untuned percussion, including vibraphone, glockenspiel, xylophone and gong (see, among many instances of this, [2], [6–8], [13], [20]). By such use of tuned percussion, the composer alerts us to the *Dream*'s magical, other-worldly dimensions, drawing on a tradition that reaches back at least as far, operatically, as Papageno's magic bells in *Die Zauberflöte* and reminding us that the dangerous attraction of Oberon is not so far removed from that of Peter Quint in *The Turn of the Screw*: both these supernatural characters share the celesta as their characterizing instrument.[6]

Act One

The structure of Act One follows an ABCBA shape of five scenes, separated by a ritornello that is first heard as a brief orchestral prelude. The ritornello device was frequently employed by Britten around the period of *A Midsummer Night's Dream*:[7] it offered a simple means of suggesting the passing of time and/or a change of location within the wood, as well as bringing musical unity across the structure of the act as a whole. Britten manipulates each of the ritornello's appearances to establish the tonality of the succeeding scene.

The act may be summarized as follows:

---

6 For a detailed interpretation of the parallels to be drawn between Quint and Oberon, see Philip Brett, 'Eros and Orientalism in Britten's Operas', in Brett, *Music and Sexuality in Britten: Selected Essays*, edited by George E. Haggerty (Berkeley: University of California Press, 2006), pp. 129–53.

7 For example, both the *Nocturne* (1958) and *Cantata Misericordium* (1963) use ritornello devices.

Ritornello

A
- Fairies
- Puck
- Oberon and Tytania
- Oberon and Puck

Ritornello

B¹   Lysander and Hermia

Ritornello (+ Oberon)

B²   Demetrius and Helena

Puck, Oberon ('I know a bank') and Ritornello

C   Rustics

Ritornello

B¹   Lysander and Hermia

B²
- Demetrius and Helena, then Helena and Lysander
- Hermia alone

Ritornello + Tytania

A
- Fairies
- Oberon

Ritornello

Britten's and Pears's jettisoning of the opening act of Shakespeare's play allowed the action of the opera to take place entirely within the wood, with the exception of the final scene of Act Three which is set in Theseus's palace. The curtain rises on the wood as twilight falls. Britten's forest murmurs to sliding divided strings (he may have been influenced here by Ravel's *L'enfant et les sortilèges*), commencing very softly in the double basses and then growing in texture, dynamics and momentum as further instruments are added. Embracing all twelve chromatic semitones, the rising and falling sonority is reminiscent of a sleeper's breathing [1]. (This is but the first example in the score of Britten's using a twelve-note procedure in a tonal rather than serial manner.) At the entrance of the first group of fairies the sliding chords have settled into an alternation of G major and F sharp major (the fairy world's key centre) over which the fairies incant 'Over hill, over dale' to a rising and falling scale in even crotchets, though their melody is unsettlingly displaced across the bar lines [2]. The cadential figure at 'We do wander everywhere' migrates to the accompaniment (bassoon) for the central section [4]. The return of the fairies' first idea completes the ternary design, but a full restatement is interrupted by the appearance of Puck for whom, after a few brisk exchanges with the fairies, Britten establishes his mischievous nature with a leaping figure on a D trumpet [5].

Oberon and Tytania enter to a slow march [6] whose descending figure on timpani becomes an important motif in their ensuing duet 'Ill met by moonlight' [7] with its arching vocal lines. Oberon and Tytania are in conflict about a human boy over whom she has possession, and their disagreement has had a detrimental effect on the natural order of things. The fundamental tonality is A major, though in Britten keys are nearly always coloured by modal inflections, as here. Moving through all twelve key centres, the duet ends with a juxtaposition of B flat minor and A major, by which semitone relationship Britten symbolically articulates the disagreement between Oberon and his queen.[8] Tytania refuses to yield the boy to Oberon

---

8   Tension between tonalities a semitone apart had been a structural feature of *Nocturne* where a conflict between C and D flat is resolved onto D flat in the final Shakespeare sonnet setting.

and she and her fairy retinue depart abruptly. Oberon resolves to punish her and calls on his helper Puck (trumpet and tabor immediately sound) to find the spellbinding herb that, when squeezed on a sleeping person's eyes, makes them fall hopelessly in love with the first creature they see on waking. A shift to E flat (a tritone away from the A major of the preceding duet) and cloying parallel major seconds on the celesta mark out Oberon's magic charm [8]. Oberon disappears and the music of the wood [1] returns in truncated form.

The first pair of lovers, Lysander and Hermia, meets in the wood. They want to marry against the wishes of Hermia's father who favours Demetrius as her suitor. They are attempting to elope but Demetrius is in pursuit, followed by Helena, whom he has jilted. In the first of the scenes between the lovers, Britten's ritornello [1] drops into C minor (though the tonality is barely ever established) for throbbing, expectant chords from the brass and aching four-note chromatic phrases from the woodwind [9] in which the lovers join [10]. These two ideas dominate the encounter which culminates in an affirmation of their love for one another against an elongated version of the throbbing motif [11]; the exchanges between Hermia and Lysander traverse all twelve keys.[9] For Britten its ending in C major symbolizes love; the minor version, however, tends to be reserved for bitter feelings between the mortals.

Following a further reprise of the wood ritornello [1] and Oberon's spell [8], Demetrius hurriedly appears in another part of the wood, his urgency felt in the syncopated accompaniment to the same chromatic phrase that dominated the first part of the scene. By employing the same material, Britten suggests the interchangeability of the pairs of lovers. Helena catches up with Demetrius, and compares herself to a fawning spaniel [12]. Once more rejecting her, Demetrius runs off, with Helena in pursuit.

Oberon has witnessed their exchange. Puck returns with the special herb which he gives to his master [8] who delivers the rapturous set piece 'I know a bank' [13]; its opening phrase is derived from the spell theme [8]. Complete with decorative harp scales and vocal

---

9   This passage was altered by the composer in his dyeline full score after he realized he had inadvertently used only eleven of the twelve triads.

melismas that bestow an impression of improvisation, this aria is Britten's tribute to Purcell. A contrasting refrain [14] sets off the decorative statements before Oberon returns to the spell theme and delivers his instructions to Puck on repeated E flats, before he and Puck disappear.

The wood ritornello returns [1], and the band of rustics enter, Bottom's characterizing trombone announcing his presence slightly ahead of the others and overlapping with the strings' glissandi [15]. The rustics have come to the wood to prepare a play to celebrate the marriage of Duke Theseus to Hippolyta. The play is to be 'Pyramus and Thisby', a tale of true love thwarted by fate, which is announced in a cadential figure that assumes significance as the scene progresses [16] and indeed later in the opera [78] when, with midnight's bell, it brings the rustics' entertainment to a conclusion. The lively *parlando* quality of this scene, full of perky rhythmic energy, recalls Britten's admiration for Verdi and one feels the influence of *Falstaff* is close at hand. Peter Quince hands out the parts and Bottom's enthusiasm gets the better of him: offered the role of Pyramus, he reveals his desire to play every part in the play, including the Lion and Thisby. Britten adumbrates many of the themes which will return in their full form (for example, [17]) when the rustics perform their play in Act Three.

The action returns to the first pair of lovers, Lysander and Hermia, who are now lost in the woods and exhausted by their journey. Britten marks the return of the lovers' music – versions of [9] with the same key signature – 'a little slower than before', because Lysander and Hermia are now weary. Their tiredness is also reflected by Britten's inverting the rhythm of the repeated chords. They lie down to sleep, articulating their goodnight 'Amens' to canonic imitation of the four-note chromatic idea over restful dominant and tonic chords in D [19]. They fall asleep. Puck enters, mistakes Lysander for Demetrius and administers the love juice to his closed eyes [20], in which the incantation music is now on Puck's trumpet in addition to arabesques on Oberon's celesta. Demetrius reappears fleetingly, and Helena, pausing for a moment from her pursuit of him, discovers Lysander and wakes him up. He declares his undying love for her, which she believes to be a trick, against impassioned rushing upward thrusts from the strings [21]. He follows her, leaving Hermia alone in the wood (versions of the two ideas in [9]).

The act concludes where it began: with Tytania and her fairy retinue. The wood music returns to the proportions and tonal centre of its initial statement to function as an accompaniment to Tytania's arioso, 'Come, now a roundel and a fairy song' [22], in which Britten exploits her vocal coloratura in delicate melodic arabesques. As she lies down to sleep her fairy guards embark on their spiky rendering of 'You spotted snakes with double tongue' [23], which begins in the fairy key of F sharp and recalls the opening scene's 'Over hill, over dale' [2] whose scalic figure is here inverted for their lullaby refrain. Oberon steals in: to his incantation music [8] he squeezes the love juice onto the sleeping Tytania's eyes. After a few further bars of the wood music, the act – and everyone in the wood – comes to rest.

Act Two

The structure of the second act is even more straightforward than the first, though less obviously schematic in arrangement. Two scenes – one for the rustics and fairies, the other for the lovers – are enclosed within a prelude and postlude and separated by an interlude, all three of which use the same material. The prelude–interlude–postlude is based on four concordant but related unmetricated chords announced at the top of the act [24] in which all twelve notes of the chromatic scale are included. Each chord employs a distinctive instrumental palette to imprint them on our aural memory: D flat major (strings), D major with an added sixth (muted brass), E flat major (woodwind) and C major (harps, harpsichord, vibraphone and suspended cymbal). The chords are clearly a homage to Mendelssohn, whose overture to his incidental music for *A Midsummer Night's Dream* begins with a four-chord motif on wind instruments. Britten was also referencing, unconsciously, as it turns out, the final song, 'Sonnet: To Sleep', from the *Serenade* for tenor, horn and strings, which begins with a virtually identical sequence of chords. (In the Keats setting from the *Serenade*, the chord sequence is: D, C sharp (= D flat),

E flat and C.) The connection was drawn to the composer's attention in 1962 by Eric Roseberry, who published his observations on the similarities between the two chord sequences in the Britten Fiftieth Birthday issue of *Tempo*.[10] Responding to a letter from Roseberry pointing out the connection, Britten wrote on 11 August 1962 that he was 'very amazed by the similarity of those MSND chords & the Serenade ones (nearly 20 years before!). I can assure you that it was purely sub-conscious! But what I think is interesting is that in the later piece I found it necessary to use *consciously* all the 12 semitones (to make each chord sound a surprise) [–] in the earlier piece it wasn't necessary. But then, the ideas were quite different – in the first a kind of harmonic overtone of the 'cello phrase, & the second, after all, theme for many variations.'[11]

The chords immediately provide the model for a sequence of four variations within which Britten introduces suggestions of the lovers' music, Oberon's spell and material associated with the rustics. It is now darkest night and Tytania is revealed sleeping. A fifth variation breaks off after the second chord as the rustics reassemble to rehearse their play [25], their appearance immediately taking up their characteristic compound time-signature and instrumental colours familiar from Act One [15]. Britten recalls other motifs characteristic of their casting scene from the earlier act as well as hinting at the full-blown parody to come when 'Pyramus and Thisby' is to be staged before the lords and ladies in the final act. Britten captures Flute's timid personality particularly well [27], in addition to his growing confidence [28]. Puck enters (trumpet). Invisible to the rustics, he observes their knockabout antics and decides to have some amusement at their expense: he transforms Bottom into an ass, complete with a triumphant glissando from the trumpet signifying his handiwork, a braying trombone for Bottom and scurrying semiquavers for the rustics' fear and confusion at this wholly unnatural sight [29]. Bottom's puzzlement at his friends' running away incorporates the obvious musical donkey joke that makes a further allusion to Mendelssohn's

---

10 Eric Roseberry, 'A Note on the Four Chords in Act II of *A Midsummer Night's Dream*', *Tempo* 66–67 (autumn–winter 1963), pp. 36–7.

11 Reed and Cooke, op. cit., p. 421.

celebrated overture [30, 31]. Alone, Bottom raises his spirits with a raucous song, 'The woosell cock' [31], which begins with a twelve-note row built around Brittenesque intervals of the second and third.

The song's lumbering gait awakens Tytania who, having been placed under the love juice's magic spell by Oberon at the conclusion of Act One, now falls in love with beast-Bottom. At her arousing (and inadvertent arousal at the sight of Bottom), Britten immediately takes us into the supernatural key of E flat (reiterated by her repetition of the key note) and the instrumental colours of the immortals [32]; the harps have a contrary-motion version of their motif from [2]. In a C major waltz-song with graceful imitation from the flute and clarinet [33], Tytania summons her four fairy attendants and instructs them to take care of Bottom's every need. Purcellian Baroque gestures are referenced in the exchange between Bottom and the fairy quartet [34] before Bottom settles himself down for the night in Tytania's arms. A drowsy B major cantilena of entwining flute and clarinet phrases over harp arpeggios presents us with some of the most beautiful music in the opera: ironically, since it accompanies a scene of such grotesquery. But Bottom is not quite ready to succumb to sleep and the opportunity for a musical entertainment from the solo fairies, one in which he might himself participate – at one point he gets up to dance – proves irresistible to him. It also allows Britten to give the boy performers a further opportunity to shine. The 'tongs and the bones', in the white-note key of C major, is scored for a pair of sopranino recorders, small cymbals and wood blocks [36]; the boys' second entertainment alludes to the nursery rhyme 'Girls and boys come out to play' without ever quite quoting it [37]; the main orchestra joins in (with a glissando snarl from the trombone) when Bottom begins to dance to the fairies' entertainment. Exhausted by these antics, he returns to Tytania's bower and her arms as she sings a lullaby to the music of [35]. At her sigh 'O how I love thee, / O how I dote on thee', the four chords [24] are recapitulated in their identical instrumental colours, to be followed by a further group of three variations – the first two with echoes of [35], the third with a rhythm associated with Puck – which functions as an interlude be-tween scenes. Just as Britten used the slithering strings as a binding ritornello in the first act, so in Act Two the four chords have a similar structural role.

The second scene opens with Puck showing Oberon the results of his work: 'This falls out better than I could devise.' Hermia and Demetrius enter: in the ensuing encounter echoes of their earlier music can be detected, most prominently the motif built around intervals of a minor third and diminished fourth [38] with quintuplet jabbing from the woodwind. She rejects him and carries on looking for Lysander while Demetrius rests for a moment. It is immediately apparent to Oberon that Puck has mismanaged his instructions and his angry 'What hast thou done?' is accompanied by E flat arabesques for the celesta. Oberon dispatches Puck to find Helena, while he anoints Demetrius's eyes with the magic juice [39] to a version of his original spell music [8].

Helena arrives pursued by Lysander, Demetrius wakes up and, to Helena's consternation, begins to woo her with impassioned arching phrases (in C minor) against an undercurrent of triplet and quaver rhythms derived from the lovers' music in Act One [40]. With Hermia's return, Helena is convinced the whole scenario has been contrived to mock and humiliate her and she turns on her old schoolfriend [41]. The rising tide of insults – as amusing in the opera as in the play – sets out from this restrained beginning to culminate in an agitated quartet of confusion [42] before the 'dwarfish' Hermia can take no more and turns the tables on Helena [43], Britten graphically portraying her carping accusations of Helena's greater physical stature with exaggeratedly wide intervals ('Now I perceive that she hath made compare / Between our statures') and a rising motif in major and minor thirds ('she hath urg'd her height'). Lysander and Demetrius challenge one another for Helena in a block-harmony derivative of the important motif of [9] and [10].

As the lovers storm off, Oberon's self-control breaks and he grabs hold of Puck – harsh, percussive chords and the glissando timpani motif from [6]. The latter motif forms an important part of his admonishing of Puck for his negligence [45]. Over an ostinato E flat pedal, he orders Puck to rectify the situation [46], a yet further variant of his incantation first heard as [8]. Puck brings down an enshrouding mist and one by one the lovers, exhausted as much by their nocturnal wanderings as by their arguments, fall asleep to the four-chord sequence [24] underpinning melodies derived from the intervals of [9] and [10]: Lysander to D flat; Demetrius to the D major with added sixth; Helena to E flat, and Hermia to the sparse C major. The chorus of fairies returns for a final lullaby ('On the ground / Sleep sound'), the melody moving in calming thirds over a four-bar rotation of the chords [47]. The tranquil mood is only momentarily disturbed when Puck squeezes the juice on Lysander's eyes, before the act ends on the D flat chord with which it began.

Act Three

Britten evokes early morning in the wood in a passage of limpid F major counterpoint for three-part divided violins [48]. This to-nality has seldom been used in the previous acts; that it comes to dominate Act Three, in which the earlier confusion is resolved, sug-gests that we should associate it with normality. The curtain rises to reveal the four lovers, Tytania and Bottom, all still asleep. Now that he has the boy who was the cause of the argument with Tytania, Oberon is ready to 'undo / This hateful imperfection of her eyes' [49], a version of [8]. Tytania awakens to the diatonic clarity of the string counterpoint which reaches a climax on an A major triad and the descending major-third tag material recalled from their scene together in Act One [50]; see also [6] and [7]. Whereas in the earlier act Britten contrived to arrange all twelve possible triads to end in a semitonal relationship symbolizing the tension between Oberon and Tytania, here he rearranges the order to reflect the fairy king and queen's new-found concord. Oberon instructs Puck to remove the ass's head from Bottom and the fairy king and queen celebrate their renewed love in a graceful sarabande [51] that is centred on E flat, the tonality associated with Oberon throughout. As the dance continues, the rest of the wood wakes up to evocations of birdsong on a pair of warbling piccolos.

The lovers awake in turn, each calling the name of their true love, to the violins' dawn music [48]. Britten hints at the mortals' return to normality by the interjection of off-stage horns calling from the world of Theseus's court [52];[12] they permeate this scene and return as an integral component in the later orchestral interlude that functions as a bridge between the wood and the court [57]. To rising scales against sustained pure major triads (Britten once again uses all twelve roots), Helena, Demetrius, Hermia and Lysander affirm their love [53]. Their previously twisting vocal lines [10] have now been straightened out, though as they leave the wood – to the words 'let us recount our dreams' – the motif from [10] is presented as a mirror canon.

Last to rouse himself is Bottom. As he comes out of his deep sleep with stretches and yawns, snatches of the play rehearsal in Act Two ('When my cue comes, call me, and I will answer') are recalled before he remembers what he believes to have been a dream [54], with appropriate musical echoes from his encounter with Tytania [30], [33], [34], [35]. His proclamation that the entire episode will be known as 'Bottom's Dream, because it hath no bottom' [55] is made to a return of the four magic chords [24]. Bottom departs with the intention of including his dream at 'the latter end of the play before the Duke', and his fellow amateur thespians rush in looking for him [56] at which point earlier material ([15] and [25]) is constantly reworked by Britten to lively effect. Bottom returns and, with 'their play preferred', the rustics embark on a bustling ensemble in preparation, with decorative coloratura from Flute, who for once seems to have forgotten his nerves.

The change of scene from the wood to Theseus's court is managed by way of a march-like interlude in which the earlier horn calls are now given full rein over a passacaglia-like bass [57] centred on F but which eventually embraces all the remaining eleven pitches. It provides a further example of Britten's lively interest, in this opera (and indeed in many of his other works from this period), in exploring dodecaphonic procedures in a purely tonal context. The interlude climaxes in one of the most lyrical utterances in all of Britten's music [58] as the duke's palace is revealed; the melody underpins Theseus's

---

12 Britten presumably took his cue from Shakespeare's stage direction: 'Horns winded within'.

words to Hippolyta. Theseus and Hippolyta receive the lovers and give them their blessing.

The rustics are called to present their play 'Pyramus and Thisby', for which Britten devises an opera-within-an-opera that parodies both nineteenth-century operatic conventions and his own structural procedures in *A Midsummer Night's Dream*, in a carefully constructed sequence of fourteen short scenes whose material has been hinted at in the rustics' casting and rehearsal scenes of the previous acts. A music-hall style fanfare [59] heralds the rustics' explanation of their announcement [60] in a parody of recitative and an imitative passage ('All for your delight') which Flute is unable to complete [61]. During the course of the play/opera, the nobles make asides in recitative ensembles in which each of the six voices moves at the natural speed of diction independently of the other voices. The entertainment begins with a Prologue from Quince [62] to introduce the characters of the play: the lovers Pyramus and Thisby, the Wall, the Moon, and the Lion. Britten makes a sly dig at *Sprechstimme* for Snout as the Wall [63], the effect exacerbated by the pedal fifths, before reaching for his main target, an affectionate rip-off of stock *bel canto* gestures [64–68], [72], [76] and circus-style music for the pantomime lion [69], [71]; even Gluck is lampooned at 'Approach, ye furies fell' [73].

Britten's decision to make a spoof *bel canto* opera for the rustics most likely stems from the success of Donizetti's *Lucia di Lammermoor* at Covent Garden in February 1959, a few months before the composer and Pears began work on the libretto. The production of *Lucia* brought soprano Joan Sutherland overnight international fame and propelled her on a subsequent career as a leading exponent of the *bel canto* repertoire. Britten had attended one of the performances of *Lucia*, which he had not much enjoyed. As he told Pears in a letter dated 27th February 1959, he found *Lucia* to be 'the most horrid experience. It is the most awful work; common & vulgar, very boring, no subtleties, poor tunes (the old Sextet is the best – Donald Duck & Clara Cluck), just as if Mozart, Gluck & all (written in 1835) hadn't existed.'[13] Specific references to Donizetti's

13 Reed and Cooke, op. cit., p. 119.

opera in 'Pyramus and Thisby' include the flute and harp of [66] and [67] (Britten obtains an additional laugh for Thisby, played by Pears in the original production, by his having deliberately to sing out of tune) and the full-blown parody of Lucia's celebrated mad scene [74], [75] in which the voice is shadowed by the flute just as it is in Donizetti's opera.[14]

An epilogue to the play is rejected by Theseus and a Bergomask based on the fanfare of [59] – now extended by playful cross-rhythms and a duple-time middle section [77] – is offered instead. Midnight sounds ([78], a version of the rustics' cadential figure in [16]) and the dancing must stop. All retire to bed and the fairy world of dreams. The low G sharps of the bell transfer five octaves upwards to the fairy tintinnabulations of the same note on the glockenspiel which resounds during the fairies' 'Now the hungry lion roars' [79]. Oberon and Tytania return to the slow march that marked their entrance in Act One [6], before they lead the fairy chorus in an ensemble in the fairy key of F sharp major built over a ground bass characterized by an inverted dotted rhythm [80]. The final word is given to Puck, his ever-spiky trumpet and tabor now supported by woodwind and strings:

> If we shadows have offended,
> Think but this (and all is mended)
> That you have but slumber'd here,
> While these visions did appear.
> Gentles, do not reprehend.
> If you pardon, we will mend.
> Else the Puck a liar call.
> So good night unto you all.
> Give me your hands, if we be friends,
> And Robin shall restore amends.

---

14 The allusion to Sutherland's Lucia was emphasized in the original English Opera Group production by Pears's acting in this scene, which evidently mimicked some of the prima donna's gestures. See Harold Rosenthal's review in *Opera* (autumn 1960), pp. 21–4, quoted in Reed and Cooke, op. cit., p. 234.

Reinventing the *Dream*:
A Midsummer Night's Dream on Stage

David Nice

Fairies and rude mechanicals once danced to the band at the Jubilee Hall, just as Sid and Nancy in *Albert Herring* had done before them, but by all accounts a good deal less comfortably given the limited space for visitors and denizens of the extra-Athenian wood. It was the world premiere of *A Midsummer Night's Dream* on 11th June 1960 and the band, even though the number of its strings had been perforce reduced in the still limited space of the renovated Aldeburgh Festival venue, was a symphony orchestra. When Britten's opera next appeared in our land, following the original English Opera Group's tour to the Holland Festival, the auditorium had a good deal more gold in it and the punters were more plentiful. This veering between intimacy and grandeur, in these cases a 341-seater and an opera house accommodating 2,000-plus (Covent Garden), has been part of the restless and often ingenious production history of the operatic *Dream* since it opened over half a century ago.

Even Britten, I suspect, would have been surprised to see his medium-sized *Dream* playing to 4,000 spectators at New York's Metropolitan Opera, as it did for the first time in 1996; on the other hand I hope he would have been delighted to see a team of Cambridge students and graduates braving it out in the tiny seating capacity of Rosslyn Chapel's mysterious forest of columns – its questionable signs and symbols unfortunately immortalized in Dan Brown's *The Da Vinci Code* – as part of the 2010 Edinburgh Festival Fringe. There was one problem with that: the last-minute fixing of a decent

41

amateur/semi-professional orchestra left the strings groaning rather more dissonantly than the composer had intended and the trumpet managing one note in a dozen as he kept falling off Puck's high wire. While I'm touching briefly on the players, the best – regardless of the conductor – must include Crispian Steele-Perkins's pit Puck alongside a woodwind department that included top oboist Nicholas Daniel and Osian Ellis as one of the two harpists under Richard Hickox in the short-lived company Opera London's staging at Sadler's Wells in 1990.

Director David Meyer's vision for that production, featuring a gigantic moon and references to the chalk giants carved into the English countryside, showed us how far we had come in terms of a *Dream* which could combine the magical and the modern. Up until then, the other great divide in productions of the Britten *Dream* has been between 'kitsch grandeur' – Sviatoslav Richter's description of the 1965 Bolshoi production, seemingly applicable to the Teatro alla Scala's 1961 Italian premiere – and a leaner, more original aesthetic: the operatic equivalent of Max Reinhardt's wildly overrated and overacted film version of Shakespeare versus the groundbreaking Peter Brook aesthetic. Or, to put it slightly differently, between pure Kensington Gardens, paraphrasing Auden's shuddering response at the Royal Opera in 1961, and Serpentine Gallery.[1]

John Piper's shimmering cloths, about which he is quoted in Andrew Plant's article, seem to have been the better part of the Cranko original production and John Gielgud's takeover for Covent Garden. But one imagines the grandeur of busy stage master Boris Pokrovsky's Moscow *mise en scène* to have been a little faded; Nicola Benois had followed his even more famous father Alexander into the world of Diaghilev's Ballets Russes before ending up at Milan's Teatro alla Scala, from where Pokrovsky borrowed him for the auspicious Soviet premiere of an acceptable Britten opera. Very much in the traditional pretty-wood vein, too, was John Copley's

---

1 'We saw BB's Midsummer Night's Dream the other day. It's dreadful! Pure Kensington.' Undated letter from W.H. Auden to Stephen Spender, Humphrey Carpenter, *W.H. Auden: A Biography* (Oxford: OUP, 1992), p. 428.

1978 Ottawa production, resuscitated in San Francisco fifteen years later.

If there is one *Midsummer Night's Dream* staged as the production-wise conservative and proprietorial Britten would have liked it which has also stood the test of time and holds its head as a viable alternative to a disparagingly titled *Regietheater*, it has to be Peter Hall's 1981 classic for Glyndebourne. The first Britten opera to be performed there since *Albert Herring* in 1947 – that too was shortly to make an unsurpassable, long-lived comeback under Hall – it immediately received the Pears seal of approval; according to Michael Kennedy, 'he told George Christie that he wished Britten had lived to see it.'[2] John Bury's stylized Elizabethan costumes, with phantasmagorical high hair for the Oberon, beautifully colour-coordinated with wood and palace; and the twinkling stars of his magical sets have sent several generations of country-house opera-goers out onto the Sussex downs hoping to see more of the same.

Only a year earlier, a disenchanting specimen of a colder alternative had made its appearance at the Snape Maltings, spacious Aldeburgh Festival alternative to the Jubilee Hall since 1967. Robin Don's triangular frame for Christopher Renshaw's version of the wood arrived at Covent Garden in 1986, at last replacing the six revivals of the Gielgud original; it was no doubt partly responsible for impressions that the score was more contrived and artificial than one had remembered. That sad state of affairs was quickly banished elsewhere, but not on the Royal Opera's main stage; in 2005 and again in 2010 in the much smaller Linbury Theatre Studio downstairs, a new production was directed by Olivia Fuchs.

Sparser dream visions had not been slow to appear. In 1961, the detail-driven Walter Felsenstein spent many months of rehearsals – a little short of the eight the Bolshoi was to demand four years later – on a Berlin Komische Oper production in marked contrast to Günther Rennert's much more lavish Hamburg premiere. The visual basis is succinctly described in *Erwin Piscator's Political Theatre: The Development of Modern German Drama* by C.D. Innes (Cambridge:

---

2   Michael Kennedy, ''Tis almost fairy time' in the Glyndebourne Festival Opera programme book 2001, p. 83.

Cambridge University Press, 1972). Here the author reflects on how the pioneering director's use of treadmills had paved the way for the 'fluidity of scene changes' in Felsenstein's *Midsummer Night's Dream,* 'where flats are hung from the grid and can be moved across the stage from above in constantly changing combinations'.

Subsequent German *Regie* productions highlighted the starker side: Willy Decker's 1986 Cologne production engaged that stunning designer John Macfarlane to project an unconventional, walled-in wood. A dark, original aspect in the physicality of the staging could still coexist with plenty of brightly coloured design. I look back to my 1983 student-newspaper review of the Scottish Opera production by John Lawson Graham and Toby Robertson – my first live acquaintance with the work – to discover that while I found the set to have 'all the garishness and evident magic of a child's picture book', the staging was 'of a more startling subtlety, notably in its handling of the sexual confusions and ambiguities'. Oberon and Puck selected young boys as they would tasty morsels; in the aftermath of the Bergomask, there was a brief orgy in which the mechanicals set upon the not-unwilling gentry.

I missed Baz Luhrmann, before he was truly famous, bringing his Opera Australia production to the 1994 Edinburgh Festival, but I well remember the excited buzz about it. Many spectators thought it was the most gorgeous thing they'd ever seen on a stage, using the 1920s Raj setting to conjure Bollywood-style blue-faced Indian gods in sexual conflict, a lurid contrast to the military uniforms of the orchestra playing on the bandstand with the magical lake on which Tytania's bower floated beneath it. Other audience members found it gimmicky and unmagical, though one who did remembers a young Ian Bostridge being perfectly cast as a floppy, tennis-playing Lysander. There's clearly still mileage to be had in the Luhrmann brand; 2010 saw revivals of the production in the major Australian cities.

The other most durable alternative to the conservative long life of the much revived Gielgud Royal Opera classic has been that of another director with an eye for unconventional visual beauty, Robert Carsen. His take was the only previous appearance of this master-piece at English National Opera and even then arriving rather late, some thirty-five years after its Aldeburgh premiere, with a production that made its first appearance at the Aix-en-Provence Festival in 1991. Bed was central to this show, possibly inspired by Jim Cartwright's National Theatre play of that name; a giant bed with a greensward counterpane yielded to six in Act Two and three for the sleeping couples suspended in mid-air at the start of Act Three (there was either a gasp or that very un-ENOish response, applause for scenery, when the curtain went up on that tableau). The magic of sleep was respected, but the joy of sex may have been a counterpoise for which the composer would not have cared; as in select theatre productions, it was the sexuality of Bottom, sporting an ass's member and an ugly head, which got comically emphasized, going against the grain of the incorruptible idyll Britten gives his big scene with Tytania. The mechanicals' play also contradicted the naivety of the composer's parodies, with stunning designs giving it more the look of experimental, sometimes surreal theatre, but it was still very funny indeed.

You'd have thought Carsen's spacious stage would have been first choice for the Metropolitan Opera's premiere staging, but that went to the equally imaginative Tim Albery in 1996, mixing periods and styles with mobster-rustics and tutued fairies – a time warp also exploited back at Aldeburgh's Jubilee Hall the following year. In Albery's stamping ground of Opera North, the Belgian-French duo of Moshe Leiser and Patrice Caurier, always ones to put on a lively show, brought a touch of weird animal magic to the fairy world, into which an evening-dressed Demetrius and Helena intruded in a sports car. This, too, was a concept older than it looked; the Britten *Midsummer Night's Dream* had been the Leiser-Caurier duo's first show together at the Opéra de Lyon back in 1983.

Beds were also among the attic bric-a-brac of Frances O'Connor's designs for Daniel Slater's Garsington production in 2010, the most recent British attempt before the 2011 ENO staging: one of the last in the enchanted gardens of the old site and going against the grain of the manicured beauty all around. A more or less alfresco *Dream* brings its problems, not least the fact that in the English summer it only begins to get dark when Shakespeare's and Britten's limpid day dawns, but Slater's show was well thought through, enterprisingly cast and in the very safe hands of a Britten protégé, Steuart Bedford, whose involvement with the opera dated back to his assistance on the 1966 Decca recording.

This brings us at last to the performers, led of course by Britten himself, who conducted the premiere before handing over later dates to George Malcolm. Solti was the choice at Covent Garden in 1961; other luminaries have included Gennady Rozhdestvensky for the Moscow premiere as well as Bernard Haitink at Glyndebourne and Sir Colin Davis, both of whom are featured in recordings (Haitink on the still-magical DVD of the original Glyndebourne production). One world-class singer seems to have softened Britten's resolve to cast a counter-tenor as Oberon. As Andrew Plant's article (pp. 19–20) makes clear, there were not only problems with Alfred Deller, the singer for whom the role had been created, but the King of the Fairies became several times a tenor in Germany (which must at least have brought him closer to the creepy-enticing world of his predecessor Peter Quint in *The Turn of the Screw*), as well as a bass – to a black Tytania in Walter Felsenstein's Komische Oper production – and a mezzo-soprano.

This last transformation clearly upset Britten the least, according to Peter Pears's diary covering their 1966 Soviet Christmas. He records his and Britten's visit to the Bolshoi to see, very reluctantly, the last act of *Madama Butterfly* with their dear friend Galina Vishnevskaya as Cio-Cio San, and 'on the stage we met the v. promising Mezzo who sings Oberon there. Unfortunately there is no performance of M.S.N.D. for another 3 weeks, long after we shall have gone.' But they were impressed with, presumably, Elena Obraztsova's Suzuki.

If mezzos ever sang Oberon again after Josephine Veasey in the 1967 Covent Garden revival, I have no record of the fact. Another departure from Britten's ideal kind of performer in a crucial role tends to have stuck. His uncharacteristic preview piece in the *Observer* on 5th June 1960 was quite clear on what he wanted from his Puck:

He seems to me to be absolutely amoral and yet innocent. In this production he is being played by the fifteen-year old son of Léonide

Massine; he doesn't sing, but only speaks and tumbles about. I got the idea of doing Puck like that in Stockholm, where I saw some Swedish child acrobats with extraordinary agility and powers of mimicry, and suddenly realised we could do Puck that way.

Unlike his father, who at a similar age had been exploited by Diaghilev as an innocent object of desire in the 1915 ballet *Josephslegende* with overblown music by Richard Strauss, Massine Junior was presumably engaged not just for his acrobatics but also for his breaking, or recently broken voice at a time when adolescents tend to give their singing voice a rest.

That's exactly the quality we hear from Stephen Terry on the 1966 recording. But more recently the operatic Puck tends to have been played as a child trapped in a man's body, or even – in the charismatic performance of Emil Wolk for Carsen – as an old-man-boy. One exception to this has been his portrayal as a pre-pubescent imp, and there can be no doubt that seven-year-old Cockney cheeky-chappy Jack Liman nearly stole the show in the 2001 Glyndebourne revival of Hall's production. Equally compelling, but in a manner undreamt of by Britten, was a young actor in the 1986 Renshaw production at Covent Garden, fresh from triumphs as the Royal Shakespeare Company's Peter Pan and Ariel. His charisma marked him out for great things – and sure enough, Mark Rylance went on to be one of the finest Hamlets (and Olivias) of his generation.

All the above have avoided the archness which is a hazard of playing Puck. We've been less lucky in truly funny Bottoms since the inimitable Owen Brannigan strutted the stage offering to play the lion's part too, though Geraint Evans must have made a resourceful alternative at Covent Garden in 1961. One rare singer today able to bring dignity as well as an acceptable degree of mugging to the role is the British bass Peter Rose. Prima-donna Tytanias since Jennifer Vyvyan have included Ileana Cotrubas in the first staging of Hall's Glyndebourne triumph, Sylvia McNair in America and, much earlier, a youngish Margaret Price when Colin Graham's new English Opera Group production was part of the opening 1967 season at the Snape Maltings (the festival that year also included the first performances of the Britten/Imogen Holst-edited Purcell *Fairy Queen*, a fascinating alternative take on Shakespeare's *Dream*).

Price as Tytania is almost as unexpected a piece of casting as Joan Sutherland playing Lady Penelope Rich in *Gloriana*; but remember both singers were at fairly early stages in their careers when they found themselves involved with a composer whose music they would perform very little subsequently. And of course we remember that both great sopranos have only recently left us. The roll call of the departed brings up other much-missed names on the British music scene, among them Susan Chilcott – a luminous Helena in the Carsen production at ENO – and Robert Tear, Snout in Britten's 1966 recording.

The roster of lovers and sub-Bottom mechanicals has featured many singers we might consider greater than their roles. Marilyn Horne sang Hermia in San Francisco's 1961 American premiere; among the lovers who have woven their way in and out of the Covent Garden woods have been Heather Harper, Janet Baker, Peter Glossop, Thomas Allen and – unforgettable for being able to urge Helena's 'tall personage' against the 'dwarfish' Hermia – Felicity Lott. Distinctive comedians in the 'tragical comedy of Pyramus and Thisby' to make their mark in the shadow of Bottom include another late, lamented singer, Donald Adams, as Quince in 1986; an equally adept Savoyard, Richard Suart, playing the Starveling in the 1990 Sadler's Wells performance; and a truly Italianate Flute to follow Pears's Sutherland-as-Donizetti-heroine spoof in the form of Barry Banks at the Met in 1996. The best news of all shows the continuing vitality of one tradition that Britten tried so hard to crank up again – the revival of the counter-tenor. Andrew Plant writes eloquently about James Bowman's stepping into the fairy shoes of Alfred Deller; the succession continued with Michael Chance, Brian Asawa, David Daniels and, most recently, Iestyn Davies in the 2011 ENO staging, all proof of the Britten–Purcell line's vibrant resuscitation.

Britten's *Dream*: An Introduction[1]

Philip Brett

When Britten turned to Shakespeare for a libretto, he was a veteran composer with six major operas and four other musico-dramatic works to his credit. The occasion for the opera was the remodelling of the tiny Jubilee Hall at Aldeburgh. Britten decided as late as August 1959 that a full-length stage work was needed to celebrate its reopening at the 1960 Festival: 'There was no time to get a libretto written,' he wrote, 'so we took one that was ready to hand.'[2] This statement can be taken with a grain of salt, for no composer's closet can have been littered with a greater number of unused libretti than his. Nor had an apparent necessity ever prevented such a decisive man from doing exactly what he pleased. The drastically truncated version of *A Midsummer Night's Dream* that Britten concocted with the help of Peter Pears answered a need by providing the composer with the opportunity to explore private concerns within a story so familiar as to divert attention away from them.

Britten, who was adept at covering his tracks, once said that *A Midsummer Night's Dream* appealed to him as the work of a very young man, and as a story that involved three different and separate groups – the lovers, the rustics (as he called the mechanicals) and the fairies – who nevertheless interact. It seems more likely that after exploring the ambiguity of relationships in a realistic setting in *Billy Budd* and the fantasy of the unthinkable in the context of

---

1 This essay first appeared in the booklet issued with the 1990 CD release of the 1966 Decca recording of the opera conducted by Britten.
2 Benjamin Britten, 'A New Britten Opera', *Observer*, 5th June 1960.

James's ghost story, *The Turn of the Screw*, the composer should have found in Shakespeare's subtle and adventurous play an ideal vehicle through which to pursue his interests in the possibilities of relationships even further.

Until after the Second World War it was common to refer to plays like *A Midsummer Night's Dream* as Shakespeare's 'romantic' or 'idyllic' comedies. Productions emphasized the magical qualities of the play, its fairy enchantment and illusion, and its romance. (Indeed, the first production of Britten's opera as designed by John Piper belonged to that tradition – another bit of camouflage.) At the time the opera was being written, however, literary critics were demonstrating that Shakespeare's comedies were saturnalian rather than romantic, and that they depended for their effect not on nineteenth-century notions of 'character' but on ritual as embodied in holiday archetypes. In *A Midsummer Night's Dream* the lovers, like celebrants on the eve of May Day, run off to the woods at night, and gain release from everyday restraint under the influence of Oberon. Both they and we gain clarification as a result. In accordance with this scheme, Shakespeare's play begins in town, in Theseus's palace, to which it returns, and which Oberon and Tytania enter, bringing blessings of fertility to the bridal couples much as country gods would bring their tribute when Elizabeth I was entertained.

As the curtain rises on Britten's opera we cannot fail to notice a crucial difference from its model. Even without the scenery, we know that we are already, in more senses than one, in the woods. It is almost impossible to resist the association with breathing and sleep, or at least with the wood as a primeval force, that is so powerfully suggested by the eerie sound of the string *portamenti*. We open at once into a world of dreams – clearly of the post-Jungian variety – which is the 'real' world of the opera. In Britten's scheme it is the court of Duke Theseus that seems unreal and limiting, the re-entry of the fairies at the end marking a return to 'normal'. In other words, Britten has simply dispensed with the social context of Athens and with the background of reality as an initiating device. He has moved here the furthest distance from the realistic borough of

Peter Grimes into a completely private world, a world of possibilities rather than of limitations. The folk festival or May games aspect of Shakespeare's play, then, has been matched by the contemporary notion of misrule, the world of the libido.

The very nature and conditions of opera, of course, go against its expression of anything so radical. Opera is after all an anachronistic performance art, set in a museum context, and patronized by a convention-loving public almost as exclusive as the aristocracy for which it was first created. Britten, however, had already shown ingenuity in injecting modern concerns into conventional formulas (most notably in *Peter Grimes*). In *A Midsummer Night's Dream* operatic convention itself becomes part of the subject of the opera.

This concern is most immediately noticeable in the broad comedy of the mechanicals' play. Pyramus and Thisby's exploration of the crudest side of nineteenth-century opera exposes them to ridicule from the audience within the opera while giving a sense of superiority to the audience without. There is a sense of wicked fun about the whole scene, from its more obvious effects to those little moments of malice, like the Schoenbergian *Sprechstimme* in which (as Peter Evans notes) Snout wails out his songs as Wall.[3] The episode clearly appealed to Britten's schoolboy sense of humour, and brought out his gift for parody. Yet his delight is tied up with a tendency of the work as a whole to parody convention in a more subtle way. As in other operas, the chorus opens *A Midsummer Night's Dream*, but it is a chorus of unbroken boys' voices, singing in unison – as different from the Romantic notion of fairies (and opera choruses) as could be imagined. Shortly after comes the expected entry of the prima donna and the male lead, who in this case is far from the ardent tenor of the Romantic era and as close as one can get nowadays to the *primo uomo* of eighteenth-century *opera seria*.

The casting of Oberon as a counter-tenor sent Britten back for models to his beloved Purcell. In Oberon's first set piece, 'I know a bank', we hear echoes of the fantastically elaborate style of Purcell's 'Sweeter than roses', which Britten had once arranged for Pears to

---

3 Peter Evans, *The Music of Benjamin Britten* (London: J.M. Dent, rev. edn., 1989), pp. 253–54.

sing. The formality of the slow march that announces the fairy king and queen and which accompanies several of their moments together also harks back to the seventeenth century. We notice that the fairy denizens of the wood, whether in Oberon's florid aria, Tytania's ecstatic 'Come now, a roundel' or the attendants' bouncy 'You spotted snakes', are much more likely to sing in rounded set pieces than the rustics or lovers who invade their territory. Theirs is a world of formality, of decorum, of a certain innocent perfection, and ultimately, of course, of nostalgia as well.

Britten's treatment of the role of Puck also suggests a difference from as well as a reference to a historical convention. The role of hero's friend or servant in opera is traditionally assigned to the baritones (e.g. in such diverse works as *Don Giovanni*, *Don Carlos* and *Tristan und Isolde*); yet Britten's Puck is a boy tumbler who speaks (in a memorable adolescent parody of baritone in the original production) rather than sings. We may remember that the rift between Oberon and Tytania is caused by Oberon's desire for 'a little changeling boy / To be my henchman'. But the fairy king already has a henchman in Puck. Theirs is the central relationship of the wood: it is certainly the one that holds the power in this labyrinth.

The appearance of a quartet of lovers who are constant in all but their affections (as Cecily puts it in *The Importance of Being Earnest*) prompts a modern audience to think almost automatically of *Così fan tutte*. Britten, however, is truer to his poet in suggesting through them the blind, irrational, compulsive state of love. These four figures tend to avoid the strings of thirds that characterize Mozart's score: they sing lines that are eternally syllabic, in even notes – a sure sign in Britten's musical language, from the archetypally syllabic Ellen Orford in *Grimes* onwards, that though conventionally 'good', there is something wrong with or limited about them. It is only after very close listening that we begin to notice the Brittenesque subtleties of characterization that distinguish them. Moreover, it is not until their awakening in Act Three that their 'unending melody' is exchanged for something like a set piece (the litany-like chorus that Britten builds out of a speech of Shakespeare's Helena, 'And I have found Demetrius like a jewel, / Mine own, and not mine own'). On the one hand this suggests that their experience in the ordered/disordered kingdom of the Dream has taught them something, but on the other it seems to consign them to a lifetime of nothing more promising than double-dating: what many modern critics and directors see as Shakespeare's gloomy prognosis for love and marriage in patriarchal society finds a modern echo in Britten's own pessimism about it.

There is one relationship in the play/opera that is purposely grotesque. Interestingly enough, Britten puts it literally at the centre of the opera, halfway through the second act, and lavishes on it some of his most luscious music. As Bottom, singing an out-of-tune song, wakes the sleeping Tytania, she bursts into a rapturous lyricism which suggests a truth that lies beyond irony. Women in Britten's operas tend to run to the extremes – they are either victims or predators. Tytania is a curious amalgam; she takes over Bottom and at the same time is utterly dominated by Oberon and Puck, whose cruel triumph (as Patricia Howard points out) eventually quells coloratura.[4] We are left at the end of the evening to ponder about the exquisite beauty of this scene.

Another episode of disquieting ambiguity occurs at the end of Act Two as Puck arranges the lovers into pairs. In the play he speaks lightly in short lines and country proverbs:

> Jack shall have Jill,
> Nought shall go ill,
> The man shall have his mare again,
> And all shall be well.

Britten gives this speech to the boy-fairies, who sing it to a shapely melody in thirds over rapturous repetitions in the orchestra of the three 'motto chords' of the act. The irony of Shakespeare is thus replaced by a statement of faith, if not quite of resolution (the final note of the melody is never vouchsafed). Sung by boys, it can only be interpreted unironically as the vision of innocence and purity that Britten seems to have tried to recapture all his life.

---

4 Patricia Howard, *The Operas of Benjamin Britten* (London: Barrie and Rockliff, 1969), pp. 169–70.

In a letter of 1942, Auden diagnosed this vision, and the attraction to 'thin-as-board-juveniles' that went with it, as a symptom of the composer's 'denial and evasion of the demands of disorder'.[5] Certainly this strange manner of quelling the libidinous activities of the forest causes concern when the glittering magic of the performance has worn off. But part of the attraction of Britten's art is the knife edge it walks between genuine feeling and the sentimental, between honesty about life's difficulties and a longing for resolution and comfort. It was not until *Owen Wingrave* (1970) and *Death in Venice* (1973) that he went on, after the ritual purification of the Church Parables (1964–68), to deal straightforwardly as well as profoundly with the two major issues of his life, pacifism and homosexual love. *A Midsummer Night's Dream* represents a stage at which he searched for the clarity that eluded him, projected a curiously ambivalent vision of the 'innocence' he could never recapture, and mulled over the nature of human relationships in a private world created out of the stuff that dreams are made on. 'He was,' Peter Pears once said when explaining Britten's dislike of 'the gay life', 'more interested in the beauty, and therefore the danger, that existed in any relationship between human beings – man and woman, man and man; the sex didn't really matter.'[6] That sex really did matter is shown, paradoxically, by the desexualizing of the creatures of the wood in *A Midsummer Night's Dream*. But it is danger, as well as beauty, that stalks through this score, and it is never quite exorcized by those fairies.

5   Donald Mitchell and Philip Reed (eds), *Letters from a Life: The Selected Letters of Benjamin Britten 1913–1976*, vol. 2 (London: Faber and Faber, 1991), pp. 1015–16.

6   In Tony Palmer's film *A Time There Was...* (1980).

A New Britten Opera[1]

Benjamin Britten

Last August it was decided that for this year's Aldeburgh Festival I should write a full-length opera for the opening of the reconstructed Jubilee Hall.

As this was a comparatively sudden decision there was no time to get a libretto written, so we took one that was ready to hand. I get a lot of letters from young people asking me how they should use their talents, and I always reply that they should try to fit them into their surroundings. This is what has happened with my new opera. It is an example of how local conditions can determine what you do.

I have always loved the *Midsummer Night's Dream*. As I get older, I find that I increasingly prefer the work either of the very young or of the very old. I always feel the *Midsummer Night's Dream* to be by a very young man, whatever Shakespeare's actual age when he wrote it. Operatically, it is especially exciting because there are three quite separate groups – the Lovers, the Rustics and the Fairies – which nevertheless interact. Thus in writing the opera I have used a different kind of texture and orchestral 'colour' for each section. For instance, the Fairies are accompanied by harps and percussion; though obviously with a tiny orchestra they can't be kept absolutely separate.

In writing opera, I have always found it very dangerous to start writing the music until the words are more or less fixed. One talks to a possible librettist, and [we] decide together the shape of the subject

---

1 This article appeared in the *Observer* on 5th June 1960, six days before the premiere of *A Midsummer Night's Dream*.

and its treatment. In my case, when I worked with E.M. Forster[2] or William Plomer,[3] for instance, we blocked the opera out in the way that an artist might block out a picture. With the *Midsummer Night's Dream*, the first task was to get it into manageable shape, which basically entailed simplifying and cutting an extremely complex story – one can only hope that one hasn't lost too much, but since the sung word takes so much longer than the spoken word, to have done the complete *Midsummer Night's Dream* would have produced an opera as long as *The Ring*.

Peter Pears (who sings Flute, the bellows-mender) and I had endless trouble with the references and the proportions of the play. We stuck faithfully to Shakespeare's words, actually adding only one line: 'Compelling thee to marry with Demetrius'. We worked from many texts, but principally from facsimiles of the First Folio and the First Quarto.

I do not feel in the least guilty at having cut the play in half. The original Shakespeare will survive. Nor did I find it daunting to be tackling a masterpiece which already has a strong verbal music of its own. Its music and the music I have written for it are at two quite different levels. I haven't tried to put across any particular idea of the play that I could equally well express in words, but although one doesn't intend to make any special interpretation, one cannot avoid it.

The opera is more relaxed than *The Turn of the Screw*; it has far more scenes, and is much less uniform. In form, it is more like *Peter Grimes*. I have felt it to be a more difficult task to write than these, partly because the work in hand is always the hardest, partly because of the tremendous challenge of those Shakespearean words. Working at it, one was very conscious that one must not let through a single ill-considered phrase because it would be matched to such great poetry.

I actually started work on the opera in October, and finished it on, I think, Good Friday – seven months for everything, including the score. This is not up to the speed of Mozart or Verdi, but these

2   Co-librettist of *Billy Budd*.
3   Librettist of *Gloriana* and the three Church Parables.

days, when the line of musical language is broken, it is much rarer. It is the fastest of any big opera I have written, though I wrote *Let's Make an Opera* in a fortnight.

Writing an opera is very different from writing individual songs: opera, of course, includes songs, but has many other musical forms and a whole dramatic shape as well. In my experience, the shape comes first. With the *Midsummer Night's Dream*, as with other operas, I first had a general musical conception of the whole work in my mind. I conceived the work without any one note being defined. I could have described the music, but not played a note.

It was a particularly bad winter for me, writing it. Normally I work perfectly regular hours, in the morning and again between four and eight. Around Aldeburgh, the weather seems always to be better in the morning; it clouds over about midday and I don't work then. I cannot work at night. In Suffolk the air is strong, and by nightfall I want to do nothing but sleep. This winter I became quite ill, but had to go on working. A lot of the third act was written when I was not at all well with flu. I didn't enjoy it. But I find that one's inclination, whether one wants to work or not, does not in the least affect the quality of the work done. Very often it is precisely after one has had what one feels to have been a wonderful morning that one needs to watch out – perhaps one's critical faculties may have been asleep.

I haven't tried to give the opera an Elizabethan flavour. It is no more Elizabethan than Shakespeare's play was Athenian. Perhaps one or two points may seem strange. The Fairies, for instance, are very different from the innocent nothings that often appear in productions of Shakespeare. I have always been struck by a kind of sharpness in Shakespeare's fairies; besides, they have some odd poetry to speak – the part about 'you spotted snakes with double tongue' for instance. The Fairies are, after all, the guards to Titania [sic]: so they have, in places, martial music. Like the actual world, incidentally, the spirit world contains bad as well as good.

Puck is a quite different character from anyone else in the play. He seems to me to be absolutely amoral and yet innocent. In this production he is being played by the fifteen-year-old son of Léonide Massine: he doesn't sing, but only speaks and tumbles about. I got the idea of doing Puck like this in Stockholm, where I saw some Swedish child acrobats with extraordinary agility and powers of mimicry, and suddenly realised we could do Puck that way.

The opera, since it was written for a hall which holds only 316 people, is small-scale. The forces one uses must necessarily be small, which has great advantages: one can work in a more detailed way with them and get a greater degree of discipline. The singers do not have to sing with such uniform volume, so that the voice can be used throughout its full range of colour. Besides, on a small scale, we can choose singers who either can act or who are prepared to learn to do so. Some opera-goers seem to prefer singers who cannot act: there is a curious inverted snobbery current in this country which even prefers operatic acting to be as bad as possible. They do not want opera to be serious at all. They like singers who merely come down to the footlights and yell.

For my part, I want singers who can act. Mozart, Gluck and Verdi wanted the same thing. There is one singer in this production who has never been on a stage before in his life;[4] but his strong concert personality fits naturally on to the operatic stage and his acting is developing very well. How many singers know how to move? I think it's essential for every potential opera singer to have a course of movement in an opera school. I must say one hoped, after the war, that audiences would revolt at seeing opera performed with bad acting, bad scenery and in a foreign language.

We are taking the *Midsummer Night's Dream* to Holland immediately after the Aldeburgh Festival. If it is any good it will get many different interpretations in many different places and all with translations. I have even heard *Peter Grimes* in Serbo-Croat. But the new opera was really written as part of the Aldeburgh Festival, for the reopening of the Jubilee Hall. Ultimately, it is to me the local things that matter most.

---

4   Alfred Deller, who created the role of Oberon, had never before performed in an opera.

Thematic Guide

Devised by Philip Reed

Themes from the opera have been identified by the numbers in square brackets in the article on the music. These are also printed at corresponding points in the libretto, so that the words can be related to the musical themes.

pale, tho - rough flood, tho - rough fire, We do wan - der eve - ry - where.

[3] FAIRIES

And we serve the Fai - ry Queen,

[4] SOLO FAIRIES

Cow - slips tall, her pen - sion - ers be,

[5]

[6] Slow march ♩ = 60

64

[70] Andante placido ♩ = 72
MOON (Starveling)
This lan - thorn doth the hor - néd Moon pre - sent.

[71] Presto feroce ♩ = 150
LION (Snug)
Oh! Oh!

[72] Lento
PYRAMUS (Bottom)
Sweet Moon, I thank thee for thy sun-ny beams,

83

A Midsummer Night's Dream

An opera in three acts
by Benjamin Britten

Libretto adapted from William Shakespeare
by Benjamin Britten and Peter Pears

A Midsummer Night's Dream was first performed at the Jubilee Hall, Aldeburgh on 11th June 1960. It was first performed in the United States at the War Memorial Opera House, San Francisco on 10th October 1961.

THE CHARACTERS

Oberon, *King of the Fairies*	counter-tenor (or contralto)
Tytania, *Queen of the Fairies*	soprano
Puck	acrobat, speaking role
Theseus, *Duke of Athens*	bass
Hippolyta, *Queen of the Amazons, betrothed to Theseus*	contralto
Lysander, *in love with Hermia*	tenor
Demetrius, *in love with Hermia*	baritone
Hermia, *in love with Lysander*	mezzo-soprano
Helena, *in love with Demetrius*	soprano
Bottom, *a weaver*	bass-baritone
Quince, *a carpenter*	bass
Flute, *a bellows-mender*	tenor
Snug, *a joiner*	bass
Snout, *a tinker*	tenor
Starveling, *a tailor*	baritone
Cobweb ⎫	treble
Peaseblossom ⎬ *Fairies*	treble
Mustardseed ⎪	treble
Moth ⎭	treble
Chorus of Fairies	trebles

A wood near Athens, then Theseus's palace

ACT ONE

The Wood, deepening twilight [1]

Enter Fairies (in two groups, Cobweb and Mustardseed with first, Peaseblossom and Moth with second).

FAIRIES
    Over hill, over dale, thorough bush, thorough brier, [2]
    Over park, over pale, thorough flood, thorough fire,
    We do wander everywhere, swifter than the Moone's sphere;
    And we serve the Fairy Queen, to dew her orbs upon the green. [3]

SOLOS
    Cowslips tall, her pensioners be, [4]
    In their gold coats, spots you see,
    Those be rubies, fairy favours,
    In those freckles live their savours.

ALL
    We must go seek some dewdrops here,
    And hang a pearl in every cowslip's ear.

PUCK *(suddenly appearing)*
    How now, spirits?

The Fairies scatter to the side.

FAIRIES
    Or I mistake your shape and making quite:
    Or are you not that shrewd and knavish sprite
    Call'd Robin Goodfellow? Are you not he, [5]
    That frights the maidens of the villagery,

Skim milk, and sometimes labour in the quern,
And bootless make the breathless huswife churn,
And sometime make the drink to bear no barm,
Mislead night-wanderers, laughing at their harm?
You do the work and they shall have good luck,
They that Hobgoblins call you, and sweet Puck!

PUCK
But room, fairy, here comes Oberon.

FAIRIES
And here our mistress;
Would that he were gone.

Enter slowly Oberon and Tytania with her train from opposite sides. [6]

FAIRIES *(whispered)*
Oberon is passing fell and wrath,
Because that she, as her attendant, hath
A lovely boy stolen from an Indian King,
And jealous Oberon would have the child.

OBERON
Ill met by moonlight, [7]
Proud Tytania.

TYTANIA
Ill met by moonlight,
Jealous Oberon. Fairies skip hence.
I have forsworn his bed and company.

The Fairies hide.

OBERON
Therefore the winds have suck'd up from the sea
Contagious fogs.

TYTANIA
Therefore the ox hath stretched his yoke in vain,

OBERON
The fold stands empty in the drowned fields,

TYTANIA
The crows are fatted with the murrion flock.

OBERON, TYTANIA
The seasons alter: the spring, the summer,
The chiding autumn, the angry winter change
Their wonted liveries, and the mazed world,
By their increase, now knows not which is which;
And this same progeny of evils comes
From our debate, from our dissention,
We are their parents and original.

OBERON
Do you amend it then, it lies in you!
Why should Tytania cross her Oberon?
I do but beg a little changeling boy,
To be my henchman.

TYTANIA
Set your heart at rest,
The Fairy land buys not the child of me.
His mother was a votress of my Order,
But she being mortal, of that boy did die,
And for her sake I will not part with him.

OBERON
Give me that boy, and I will go with thee.

TYTANIA
Not for thy Fairy kingdom. Fairies away!

Exit Tytania with Fairies.

OBERON
Well, go thy way: thou shalt not from this grove,
Till I torment thee for this injury.
My gentle Puck come hither; thou rememb'rest   [8]
The herb I shewed thee once;

91

The juice of it, on sleeping eye-lids laid,
Will make or man or woman madly dote
Upon the next live creature that it sees,
(Be it on Lion, Bear, or Wolf, or Bull,
On meddling Monkey, or on busy Ape).
Fetch me this herb, and be thou here again,
Ere the leviathan can swim a league.

PUCK
I'll put a girdle round about the earth,
In forty minutes.

Puck flies off.

OBERON
Having once this juice,
I'll watch Tytania, when she is asleep,
And drop the liquor of it in her eyes:
And ere I take this charm from off her sight
I'll make her render up her page to me.

Oberon disappears.

Enter Lysander and Hermia, separately, meeting.   [9]

LYSANDER
How now my love? Why is your cheek so pale?   [10]
How chance the roses there do fade so fast?

HERMIA
Belike for want of rain, which I could well
Beteem them from the tempest of my eyes.

LYSANDER
Aye me; for aught that I could ever read,
Could ever hear by tale or history,
The course of true love never did run smooth,
But either it was different in blood –

HERMIA, LYSANDER
O cross!

HERMIA
Too high to be enthrall'd to low.

LYSANDER
Or else misgraffed, in respect of years –

HERMIA, LYSANDER
O spite!

HERMIA
Too old to be engag'd to young.

LYSANDER
Or else it stood upon the choice of friends.

HERMIA, LYSANDER
O hell!

HERMIA
To choose love by another's eyes.

HERMIA, LYSANDER
If then true lovers have been ever cross'd,
It stands as an edict in destiny –

HERMIA
Then let us teach our trial patience.

LYSANDER
A good persuasion; therefore hear me Hermia,
I have a widow aunt, a dowager,
Of great revenue, and she hath no child:
From Athens is her house remote seven leagues,
And she respects me, as her only son.
There gentle Hermia, may I marry thee,
And to that place, the sharp Athenian Law
(Compelling thee to marry with Demetrius)
Cannot pursue us. If thou lov'st me, then
There will I go with thee.

HERMIA
  My good Lysander, (if thou lov'st me)
  I swear to thee, by Cupid's strongest bow,   [11]

LYSANDER
  I swear to thee,
  By his best arrow with the golden head,

HERMIA
  I swear to thee,
  By the simplicity of Venus' doves,

LYSANDER
  I swear to thee
  By that which knitteth souls, and prospers loves,

HERMIA, LYSANDER
  And by that fire which burn'd the Carthage Queen,
  When the false Troyan under sail was seen,

HERMIA
  By all the vows that ever men have broke,

LYSANDER
  In number more than ever women spoke,

HERMIA, LYSANDER
  I swear to thee...

Exeunt.

The wood is empty.   [1]

Enter Oberon.

OBERON
  (Be it on Lion, Bear or Wolf, or Bull,   [8]
  On meddling Monkey, or busy Ape).
  But who comes here? I am invisible;
  I will overhear their conference.

Enter Demetrius, Helena pursuing him.

DEMETRIUS
    I love thee not, therefore pursue me not,   [9]
    Where is Lysander, and fair Hermia?
    The one I'll slay, the other slayeth me.
    Thou told'st me they were stol'n unto this wood:
    And here am I, and wode within this wood,
    Because I cannot meet my Hermia.
    Hence, get thee gone, and follow me no more.

HELENA *(panting)*
    You draw me, you hard-hearted adamant,
    Leave you your power to draw,
    And I shall have no power to follow you.

DEMETRIUS
    Do I entice you? Do I speak you fair?
    Or rather do I not in plainest truth,
    Tell you I do not, nor I cannot love you?

HELENA
    And even for that do I love you the more;
    I am your spaniel, and Demetrius,   [12]
    The more you beat me, I will fawn on you.
    Use me but as your spaniel; spurn me, strike me,
    Neglect me, lose me; only give me leave
    (Unworthy as I am) to follow you.

DEMETRIUS
    Tempt not too much the hatred of my sprite,   [9]
    For I am sick when I do look on thee.

HELENA
    And I am sick when I look not on you.

DEMETRIUS
    I'll run from thee, and hide me in the brakes,
    And leave thee to the mercy of wild beasts.

Exit Demetrius.

HELENA
I'll follow thee, and make a heaven of hell,
To die upon the hand I love so well.

Exit Helena.

OBERON
Fare thee well nymph, ere he do leave this grove,
Thou shalt fly him, and he shall seek thy love.

Puck flies in.

Welcome wanderer. Hast thou the flower there?

Puck gives him the flower and lies at his feet.   [8]

OBERON
I know a bank where the wild thyme blows,   [13]
Where Oxlips and the nodding Violet grows,
Quite over-canopied with luscious Woodbine,
With sweet musk-roses, and with Eglantine;
There sleeps Tytania, sometime of the night,   [14]
Lull'd in these flowers, with dances and delight:
And there the snake throws her enammel'd skin,
Weed wide enough to wrap a Fairy in.
And with the juice of this I'll streak her eyes,
And make her full of hateful fantasies.   [8]
Take thou some of it, and seek through this grove;
A sweet Athenian lady is in love
With a disdainful youth: annoint his eyes,
But do it when the next thing he espies
May be the Lady. Thou shalt know the man
By the Athenian garments he hath on.

Exeunt Oberon and Puck.

The wood is left empty.   [1]

The six rustics enter cautiously.   [15]

QUINCE
Is all our company here?

96

ALL

Ay. Ay.

BOTTOM

You were best to call them generally, man by man, according to
the scrip.

FLUTE

First, good Peter Quince, say what the play treats on.

QUINCE

Marry our play is the most lamentable comedy, and most cruel
death of Pyramus and Thisby.   [16]

ALL

Of Pyramus and Thisby.

BOTTOM

A very good piece of work I assure you, and a merry. Now good
Peter Quince, call forth your actors by the scroll. Masters spread
yourselves.

QUINCE

Answer as I call you. Nick Bottom the weaver.

BOTTOM

Ready; name what part I am for, and proceed.

QUINCE

You Nick Bottom are set down for Pyramus.

BOTTOM

What is Pyramus, a lover or a tyrant?

QUINCE

A lover that kills himself most gallant for love.

BOTTOM

My chief humour is for a tyrant. I could play Ercles rarely, or
a part to tear a cat in, to make all split the raging rocks; and
shivering shocks shall break the locks of prison-gates, and
Phibbus' car shall shine from far, [17] and make and mar the

foolish Fates. This was lofty. Now name the rest of the players. This is Ercles' vein, a tyrant's vein: a lover more condoling.

QUINCE
Francis Flute the bellows-mender.

FLUTE
Here, Peter Quince.

QUINCE
Flute, you must take Thisby on you.

FLUTE
What is Thisby, a wandering knight? [18]

QUINCE
It is the lady that Pyramus must love.

FLUTE
Nay faith, let not me play a woman, I have a beard coming.

QUINCE
That's all one, you shall play it in a mask, and you may speak as small as you will.

BOTTOM
An I may hide my face, let me play Thisby too: I'll speak in a monstrous little voice: 'Thisne, Thisne,' 'Ah Pyramus my lover dear, thy Thisby dear, and Lady dear.'

QUINCE
No, no, you must play Pyramus, and Flute you Thisby.

BOTTOM
Well, proceed.

FLUTE (practising)
('Ah Pyramus my lover dear, thy Thisby dear, and Lady…') [27]

QUINCE
Robin Starveling the tailor.

STARVELING

Here, Peter Quince.

QUINCE

Robin Starveling, you must play Thisby's mother. Tom Snout the tinker.

SNOUT

Here, Peter Quince.

QUINCE

You, Pyramus' father; myself, Thisby's father; Snug the joiner, you the Lion's part: and I hope here is a play fitted.

SNUG

Have you the Lion's part written? Pray you if be, give it me, for I am slow of study. [16]

QUINCE

You may do it extempore, for it is nothing but roaring.

BOTTOM

Let me play the Lion too, I will roar that I will do any man's heart good to hear me. I will roar, that I will make the Duke say, Let him roar again, let him roar again.

FLUTE

And you should do it too terribly, you would fright the Duchess and the Ladies, that they would shriek, and that were enough to hang us all.

ALL

That would hang us every mother's son.

BOTTOM

But I will aggravate my voice so, that I will roar you as gently as any sucking dove; I will roar you and 'twere any nightingale.

QUINCE

You can play no part but Pyramus, for Pyramus is a sweet-fac'd man, a proper man, and most lovely gentleman-like man, therefore you must needs play Pyramus.

BOTTOM
Well, I will undertake it.

General satisfaction.

QUINCE
But masters here are your parts, and I am to entreat you, request you, and desire you, to con them by tonight; here will we rehearse anon.

BOTTOM
We will meet, and here we may rehearse most obscenely and courageously. Take pains, be perfect, adieu.

ALL
Adieu, adieu.

QUINCE
Adieu, at the Duke's oak we meet.

ALL
Adieu, adieu.

Exeunt.

The wood is left empty.   [1]

Enter Lysander and Hermia.   [9]

LYSANDER
Fair love, you faint with wandering in the wood,
And to speak troth I have forgot our way:
We'll rest us Hermia, if you think it good,
And tarry for the comfort of the day.

HERMIA
Be it so Lysander; find you out a bed,
For I upon this bank will rest my head.

LYSANDER
One turf shall serve as pillow for us both,
One heart, one bed, two bosoms, and one troth.

HERMIA
    Nay good Lysander, for my sake my dear
    Lie further off yet, do not lie so near.
    So far be distant, and good night sweet friend;
    Thy love ne'er alter, till thy sweet life end.

LYSANDER
    Amen, amen, to that fair prayer, say I,   [19]
    And then end life, when I end loyalty:

HERMIA
    Amen, amen, say I.
    And then end life, when I end loyalty.

They sleep. Enter Puck.

PUCK
    Through the forest have I gone,   [5]
    But Athenian found I none,
    On whose eyes I might approve
    This flower's force in stirring love.
    Night and silence; who is here?
    Weeds of Athens he doth wear:
    This is he (my master said)
    Despised the Athenian maid:

He squeezes the juice on Lysander's eyes.

    Churl, upon thy eyes I throw   [20]
    All the power this charm doth owe:
    So awake when I am gone:
    For I must now to Oberon.

HERMIA *(in her sleep)*
    Amen to that fair prayer, say I.   [19]

Exit Puck.

Enter Demetrius and Helena running.

HELENA
    Stay, though thou kill me, sweet Demetrius.   [9]

DEMETRIUS

I charge thee hence, and do not haunt me thus.

HELENA

O wilt thou darkling leave me? do not so.

DEMETRIUS

Stay on thy peril, I alone will go.

Exit Demetrius.

HELENA

O I am out of breath, in this fond chase,
The more my prayer, the lesser is my grace,
Happy is Hermia, whereso'er she lies;
For she hath blessed and attractive eyes.
Alas, I am as ugly as a bear;
For beasts that meet me, run away for fear.
But who is here? Lysander on the ground;
Dead or asleep? I see no blood, no wound,
Lysander, if you live, good sire awake.

Lysander awakes.

LYSANDER

And run through fire I will for thy sweet sake. [21]
Transparent Helena, Nature shows her art,
That through thy bosom makes me see thy heart.
Where is Demetrius? O how fit a word
Is that vile name, to perish on my sword!

HELENA

Do not say so Lysander, say not so:
What though he love your Hermia? Lord, what though?
Yet Hermia still loves you; then be content.

LYSANDER

Content with Hermia? No, I do repent
The tedious minutes I with her have spent.
Not Hermia, but Helena I love;
Who will not change a raven for a dove?

HELENA

    Wherefore was I to this keen mockery born?
    When at your hands did I deserve this scorn?
    Good troth you do me wrong (good sooth you do)
    In such disdainful manner, me to woo.
    But fare you well; perforce I must confess,
    I thought you Lord of more true gentleness.

Exit Helena.

LYSANDER

    She sees not Hermia: Hermia sleep thou there,
    And never mayst thou come Lysander near;
    And all my powers address your love and might,
    To honour Helen, and to be her knight.

Exit Lysander.

HERMIA *(waking)*

    Help me Lysander, what a dream was here,   [9]
    Lysander look, how I do quake with fear:
    Methought a serpent eat my heart away,
    And you sat smiling at his cruel prey.

(looking around)

    Lysander, what remov'd? Lysander, Lord,
    What, out of hearing, gone? No sound, no word?
    Alack where are you? Speak and if you hear:
    Speak of all loves; I swoon almost with fear.
    Lysander, Lord...

Exit Hermia.

*Enter Tytania, Queen of Fairies, with Cobweb, Peaseblossom,
Mustardseed, Moth and other Fairies.*

TYTANIA *(distant)*

    Come, now a roundel, and a fairy song;   [22]
    Then for the third part of a minute, hence,
    Some to kill cankers in the musk-rose buds,
    Some war with reremice, for their leathern wings,

(entering)

> To make my small elves coats, and some keep back
> The clamorous owl that nightly hoots and wonders
> At our quaint spirits: sing me now asleep,
> Then to your offices, and let me rest.

She lies down with the Fairies around her.

SOLO FAIRIES
> You spotted snakes with double tongue,   [23]
> Thorny hedgehogs be not seen,
> Newts and blind-worms do no wrong,
> Come not near our Fairy Queen.
> Philomel with melody,
> Sing in our sweet lullaby.

ALL
> Lulla, lulla, lullaby, lulla, lulla, lullaby,   [2]
> Never harm, nor spell, nor charm,
> Come our lovely Lady nigh.
> So good night with lullaby.

SOLO FAIRIES
> Weaving spiders come not here,   [23]
> Hence you long-legg'd spinners, hence;
> Beetles black approach not near;
> Worm nor snail do no offence.
> Philomel with melody,
> Sing in our sweet lullaby.

ALL
> Lulla, lulla, lullaby, lulla, lulla, lullaby,   [2]
> Never harm, nor spell, nor charm,
> Come our lovely Lady nigh.
> So good night with lullaby.

COBWEB
> Hence away, now all is well;   [23]
> One aloof, stand sentinel.

Tytania sleeps. The Fairies except one standing sentry slip out.
Enter Oberon.

OBERON
  What thou seest when thou dost wake,   [8]
  Do it for thy true Love take:
  Love and languish for his sake.
  Be it ounce, or cat, or bear,
  Pard, or boar with bristled hair,
  In thy eye that shall appear,
  When thou wak'st, it is thy dear,
  Wake when some vile thing is near.

He squeezes the juice on Tytania's eyes and disappears.

(Curtain)   [1]

ACT TWO

The Wood, dark night   [24]

Tytania lying asleep.

Enter the six rustics.   [25]

BOTTOM
　　Are we all met?

THE OTHERS
　　Pat, pat.

QUINCE
　　And here's a marvellous convenient place for our rehearsal.

THE OTHERS
　　For our rehearsal.

BOTTOM
　　Peter Quince?

QUINCE
　　What sayest thou, bully Bottom?

BOTTOM
　　There are things in this comedy that will never please. First,
　　Pyramus must draw a sword to kill himself, which the Ladies
　　cannot abide.

THE OTHERS
　　By'r lakin, a parlous fear.

FLUTE

I believe we must leave the killing out, when all is done.

BOTTOM

Not a whit, I have a device to make all well. Write me a Prologue; tell them, that I Pyramus am not Pyramus, but Bottom the weaver; this will put them out of fear.

SNUG

Will not the Ladies be afear'd of the Lion?

THE OTHERS

The Lion.

FLUTE

I fear it, I promise you.

BOTTOM

Therefore another Prologue must tell them plainly he is not a Lion but Snug the joiner.

QUINCE

But there is two hard things, that is, to bring the moonlight into a chamber: for you know Pyramus and Thisby meet by moonlight.

STARVELING

Doth the moon shine that night we play our play?

BOTTOM

A Calendar, a Calendar, look in the Almanac, find out moonshine, find out moonshine.

THE OTHERS

Moonshine, moonshine.

BOTTOM

Or else one must come in with a bush of thorns and a lanthorn and say he comes to present the person of Moonshine.

THE OTHERS

Moonshine.

QUINCE
  Then there is another thing, we must have a wall in the great chamber.

SNOUT
  You can never bring in a wall.

ALL
  What say you Bottom?

BOTTOM
  Some man or other must present wall, and let him hold his fingers thus, and through that cranny shall Pyramus and Thisby whisper.

THE OTHERS
  Then all is well.

QUINCE
  Come, sit down every mother's son, and rehearse your parts, every man according to his cue. Pyramus, you begin.   [15]

Puck flies in.

PUCK
  What hempen home-spuns have we swaggering here   [5]
  So near the cradle of the Fairy Queen?

QUINCE
  Speak Pyramus: Thisby stand forth.

BOTTOM *(as Pyramus)*
  Thisby, the flowers of odious savours sweet...

QUINCE
  Odours, odorous.

BOTTOM *(as Pyramus)*
  Odours savours sweet,
  So hath thy breath, my dearest Thisby dear.
  But Hark, a voice; stay thou but here a while   [26]
  And by and by I will to thee appear.

Exit Bottom.

PUCK
I'll follow you, I'll lead you about a round.   [5]

Exit Puck.

FLUTE
Must I speak now?

QUINCE
Ay marry must you. For you must understand he goes but to see
a noise he heard and is to come again.

FLUTE *(as Thisby)*
Most radiant Pyramus, most lily-white of hue,   [27]
Of colour like the red rose on triumphant brier,
Most brisky juvenal, and eke most lovely Jew,   [28]
As true as truest horse, that yet would never tire,
I'll meet thee, Pyramus, at Ninny's tomb.

QUINCE
Why, you must not speak that yet; that you answer to Pyramus:
you speak all your part at once, cues and all. Pyramus enter, your
cue is past, it is 'never tire'.

FLUTE *(as Thisby)*
O, as true as truest horse, that yet would never tire.

Enter Puck and Bottom with the ass-head.

BOTTOM *(as Pyramus)*
If I were fair, Thisby, I were only thine.

Exit Puck.

THE OTHERS
O monstrous, O strange. We are haunted, pray masters, fly
masters, help.   [29]

Exeunt Flute, Snout, Starveling, Quince and Snug.

BOTTOM

Why do they run away? this is a knavery to make me afeard. [30]

Flute reappears.

FLUTE

O Bottom, thou art chang'd; what do I see on thee?

Exit Flute.

BOTTOM

What do you see? You see an ass-head of your own, do you?

The rustics reappear from behind the trees.

ALL

Bless thee, Bottom, bless thee; thou art translated.

Exeunt.

BOTTOM

I see their knavery; this is to make an ass of me, to fright me, if
they could; but I will not stir from this place, and I will sing that
they shall hear I am not afraid.

The woosell cock, so black of hue   [31]
With orange-tawny bill,
The throstle, with his note so true,
The wren, with little quill…

TYTANIA *(awakening)*

What angel wakes me from my flowery bed?   [32]

BOTTOM

The finch, the sparrow, and the lark,   [31]
The plain-song cuckoo grey
Whose note full many a man doth mark
And dares not answer, nay.

TYTANIA

I pray thee gentle mortal, sing again;   [32]
Mine ear is much enamour'd of thy note;

So is mine eye enthralled to thy shape,
Thou art as wise, as thou art beautiful.

BOTTOM
    Not so neither, but if I had wit enough to get out of this
    wood…

TYTANIA
    Out of this wood do not desire to go,
    Thou shalt remain here, whether thou wilt or no.
    I am a spirit of no common rate;
    I'll give thee Fairies to attend on thee;
    Peaseblossom, Cobweb, Moth and Mustardseed!

Enter Peaseblossom, Cobweb, Moth and Mustardseed.

PEASEBLOSSOM
    Ready.

COBWEB
        And I.

MOTH
            And I.

MUSTARDSEED
            And I.

ALL FOUR
    Where shall we go?

TYTANIA
    Be kind and courteous to this gentleman,   [33]
    Hop in his walks and gambol in his eyes,
    Feed him with apricocks, and dewberries,
    With purple grapes, green figs, and mulberries,
    The honey-bags steal from the humble bees,
    And for night-tapers crop their waxen thighs,
    And light them at the fiery glow-worms' eyes,
    To have my love to bed, and to arise:
    Nod to him elves, and do him courtesies.

ALL FOUR FAIRIES *(bowing to Bottom)*
    Hail mortal, hail!   [34]

BOTTOM
    I cry your worship's mercy heartily; I beseech your worship's
    name.

COBWEB
    Cobweb. Hail mortal, hail.

BOTTOM
    I shall desire you of more acquaintance, good Master Cobweb.
    Your name, honest gentleman?

PEASEBLOSSOM
    Peaseblossom. Hail, mortal, hail.

BOTTOM
    I pray you commend me to Mistress Squash, your mother, and to
    Master Peascod your father. Your name, I beseech you, sir?

MUSTARDSEED
    Mustardseed. *(with the others)* Hail mortal, hail.

BOTTOM
    Your kindred hath made my eyes water, ere now. Good Master
    Mustardseed, I desire you more acquaintance. Your name, sir?

MOTH
    M...

TYTANIA *(interrupting)*
    Come, sit thee down upon this flowery bed
    While I thy amiable cheeks do coy,
    And stick musk-roses in thy sleek smooth head,
    And kiss thy fair large ears, my gentle joy.

Tytania and Bottom settle down on the bank.   [35]

BOTTOM
    Where's Peaseblossom?

PEASEBLOSSOM
Ready.

BOTTOM
Scratch my head, Peaseblossom. Where's Mounsieur Cobweb?

COBWEB
Ready.

BOTTOM
Mounsieur Cobweb, get your weapons in your hand, and kill me a red-hipped humble-bee, and good Mounsieur, bring me the honey-bag. Where's Mounsieur Mustardseed?

MUSTARDSEED
Ready.

BOTTOM
Give me your neaf, Mounsieur Mustardseed. Pray you leave your courtesy good Mounsieur.

MUSTARDSEED
What's your will?

BOTTOM
Nothing, good Mounsieur, but to help Cavalery Cobweb to scratch. I am such a tender ass, if my hair do but tickle me, I must scratch. Where's Mounsieur Moth?

MOTH
H…

TYTANIA *(interrupting)*
What, wilt thou hear some music, my sweet love?

BOTTOM
I have a reasonable good ear in music.
Let's have the tongs and the bones.

The Fairies take their instruments, recorders and percussion, and start to play.   [36]

I have a reasonable good ear in music.

More music. Bottom gets up and begins to dance. [37]

    But I pray you let none of your people stir me, [35]
    I have an exposition of sleep come upon me.

TYTANIA
    Sleep thou, and will wind thee in my arms.
    Fairies begone, and be all ways away.

Exeunt Fairies.

TYTANIA
    So doth the woodbine, the sweet Honeysuckle
    Gently entwist; the female ivy so
    Enrings the barky fingers of the Elm.
    O how I love thee! How I dote on thee! [24]

They sleep, and it grows dark.

Enter Oberon and Puck severally.

OBERON
    How now, mad spirit,
    What night-rule now about this haunted grove?

PUCK
    See, my Mistress with a monster is in love.

OBERON
    This falls out better than I could devise.
    But hast thou yet latch'd the Athenian's eyes
    With a love-juice, as I did bid thee do?

Enter Hermia and Demetrius.

Stand close, this is the same Athenian.

PUCK
    This is the woman, but not this the man.

They listen.

DEMETRIUS
    O why rebuke you him that loves you so? [38]

HERMIA
If thou hast slain Lysander in his sleep,
Plunge in the deep, and kill me too:
Ah good Demetrius, wilt thou give him me?

DEMETRIUS
I'd rather give his carcase to my hounds.

HERMIA
Out dog, out cur, oh hast thou slain him then?

DEMETRIUS
I am not guilty of Lysander's blood.

HERMIA
I pray thee tell me then that he is well.

DEMETRIUS
And if I could, what should I get therefore?

HERMIA
A privilege, never to see me more;
And from thy hated presence part I so;
See me no more, whether he be dead or no.

Exit Hermia.

DEMETRIUS
There is no following her in this fierce vein,
Here therefore for a while I will remain.
So sorrow's heaviness doth heavier grow.

Lies down.

OBERON
What hast thou done? Thou hast mistaken quite
And laid the love-juice on some true-love's sight;
About the wood go swifter than the wind,
And Helena of Athens look thou find.

PUCK
I go, I go, look how I go,
Swifter than an arrow from the Tartar's bow.

Puck flies off.

OBERON *(squeezing flower on to Demetrius' eyes)*
    Flower of this purple dye,   [39]
    Hit with Cupid's archery,
    Sink in apple of his eye,
    When his love he doth espy,
    Let her shine as gloriously
    As the Venus of the sky.
    When thou wak'st if she be by
    Beg of her for remedy.

Puck flies in.

PUCK
    Captain of our fairy band,
    Helena is here at hand,
    And the youth, mistook by me;
    Shall we their fond pageant see?
    Lord, what fools these mortals be!

Oberon and Puck stand aside.

Enter Lysander and Helena.

LYSANDER
    Why should you think that I should woo in scorn?

HELENA
    These vows are Hermia's. Will you give her o'er?

LYSANDER
    I had no judgement, when to her I swore.

HELENA
    Nor none in my mind, now you give her o'er.

LYSANDER
    Demetrius loves her, and he loves not you.

Demetrius awakes.

DEMETRIUS

    O Helen, goddess, nymph, perfect, divine,   [40]
    To what my love shall I compare thine eyne?
    Crystal is muddy. O how ripe in show
    Thy lips, these kissing cherries, tempting grow!
    That pure congealed white, high Taurus' snow
    Fann'd with the eastern wind, turns to a crow,
    When thou hold'st up thy hand. O let me kiss
    This Princess of pure white, this seal of bliss.

HELENA

    O spite! O hell! I see you all are bent
    To set against me, for your merriment.

LYSANDER

    You are unkind, Demetrius; be not so,
    For you love Hermia; this you know I know.

DEMETRIUS

    Look where thy love comes, yonder is thy dear.

Enter Hermia.

HERMIA

    Lysander, why unkindly didst thou leave me so?

HELENA

    Injurious Hermia, most ungrateful maid,
    Have you conspir'd, have you with these contriv'd
    To bait me with this foul derision?
    Is all the counsel that we two have shar'd,
    The sisters' vows, the hours that we have spent,
    When we have chid the hasty-footed time
    For parting us; O is all forgot?   [41]
    All school-days friendship, childhood innocence?
    We, Hermia, like to artificial gods,
    Have with our needles created one flower,
    Both on one sampler, sitting on one cushion,
    Both warbling of one song, both in one key;
    Two lovely berries, moulded on one stem,
    So with two seeming bodies, but one heart.

And will you rend our ancient love asunder,
To join with men in scorning your poor friend?
It is not friendly, 'tis not maidenly.

HERMIA
I am amazed at your passionate words.
I scorn you not: it seems that you scorn me.

HELENA
Ay do, persever, counterfeit sad looks,
Make mouths upon me when I turn my back,
Wink at each other, hold the sweet jest up:
But fare ye well, 'tis partly my own fault,
Which death or absence soon shall remedy.

LYSANDER
Stay, gentle Helena, hear my excuse,
My love, my life, my soul, fair Helena.

HELENA
O excellent!

[42]

HERMIA *(to Lysander)*
Sweet, do not scorn her so.

DEMETRIUS
If she cannot entreat, I can compel.

LYSANDER
Thou canst compel, no more than she entreat.

DEMETRIUS
I say, I love her more than you can do.

LYSANDER
If thou say so, withdraw and prove it too.

DEMETRIUS
Quick, come.

HERMIA *(holds Lysander)*
Lysander, whereto tends all this?

LYSANDER
Away, you Ethiope.

DEMETRIUS
No, no, sir, seem to break loose:
You are a tame man, go.

LYSANDER *(shaking off Hermia)*
Hang off, thou cat, thou burr, vile thing, let loose,
Or I will shake thee from me like a serpent.

HERMIA
Why are you grown so rude?
What change is this, sweet love?

LYSANDER
Thy love? Out, tawny Tartar, out;
Out, loathed medicine: hated potion, hence.

HERMIA
Do you not jest?

HELENA
Yes, sooth, and so do you.

DEMETRIUS
Demetrius, I will keep my word with thee.

DEMETRIUS
I would I had your bond.
I'll not trust your word.

LYSANDER
What, should I hurt her, strike her, kill her dead?
Although I hate her, I'll not harm her so.

HERMIA
What, can you do me greater harm than hate?
Am I not Hermia? Are not you Lysander?

DEMETRIUS
Lysander, keep thy Hermia, I will none.
If e'er I loved her all that love is gone.

LYSANDER

Ay, by my life; be certain 'tis no jest,
That I do hate thee and love Helena.

HELENA

You both are rivals and love Hermia,
And now are rivals to mock Helena.

HERMIA *(to Helena)*

O me, you juggler, you canker-blossom,
You thief of love.

HELENA

Fie, fie, you counterfeit, you puppet, you.

HERMIA

Puppet? why so? ay, that way goes the game.   [43]
Now I perceive that she hath made compare
Between our statures; she hath urg'd her height,
And with her personage, her tall personage,
Her height (forsooth) she hath prevail'd with him.
And are you grown so high in his esteem,
Because I am so dwarfish and so low?
How low am I, you painted maypole? Speak,
How low am I? I am not yet so low
But that my nails can reach unto thine eyes.

HELENA

I pray you though you mock me, gentlemen,
Let her not hurt me; you perhaps may think,
Because she is something lower than myself,
That I can match her.

HERMIA

Lower? Hark again.

HELENA

O when she's angry, she is keen and shrewd,   [44]
She was a vixen when she went to school,
And though she be but little, she is fierce.

HERMIA
Little again? Nothing but low and little?

HELENA
Get you gone, you dwarf,
You *minimus* of hindering knot-grass made,
You bead, you acorn.

HERMIA
Hark again.
Why will you suffer her to flout me thus?
Let me come to her.

LYSANDER
Be not afraid, she shall not harm thee, Helena.

DEMETRIUS
No sir, she shall not, though you take her part.

LYSANDER
You are too officious
In her behalf that scorns your services.

DEMETRIUS
Let her alone; speak not of Helena.

LYSANDER
Now follow if thou darest, to try whose right
Of thine or mine is most in Helena.

DEMETRIUS
Nay, I'll go with thee cheek by jowl to try whose right
Of thine or mine is most in Helena.

Exeunt Lysander and Demetrius.

HERMIA
You, mistress, all this coil is 'long of you
Nay, go not back.
Nor longer stay in your curst company.

HELENA

You, mistress, all this coil is 'long of you
I will not trust you, I,
Nor longer stay in your curst company.
Your hands than mine are quicker for a fray,
My legs are longer though to run away.

Exit Helena pursued by Hermia.

Oberon comes forward in a rage, dragging Puck.

OBERON

This is thy negligence, still thou mistak'st,   [45]
Or else committ'st thy knaveries wilfully.

PUCK

Believe me, King of shadows, I mistook.

OBERON

Thou see'st these lovers seek a place to fight;
Hie therefore Robin, overcast the night,
And lead these testy rivals so astray
As one come not within another's way.
Till o'er their brows, death-counterfeiting sleep   [46]
With leaden legs and batty wings doth creep;
Then crush this herb into Lysander's eye.
When they next wake, all this derision
Shall seem a dream, and fruitless vision.
Haste, Robin, haste, make no delay;
We may effect this business yet, ere day.

Oberon vanishes.

A mist descends.

PUCK

Up and down, up and down   [5]
I will lead them up and down:
I am fear'd in field and town.
Goblin, lead them up and down.
Here comes one.

LYSANDER *(distant)*
  Where art thou, proud Demetrius? Speak thou now.

PUCK *(imitating Demetrius)*
  Here, villain, drawn and ready. Where art thou?
  Follow me then to plainer ground.

DEMETRIUS *(distant)*
  Lysander, speak again.
  Thou runaway, thou coward, art thou fled?

PUCK *(imitating Lysander)*
  Art bragging to the stars and wilt not come?

DEMETRIUS
  Yea, art thou there?

PUCK
  Follow my voice, we'll try no manhood here.

Exit.

Enter Lysander.

LYSANDER
  He goes before me, and still dares me on.

PUCK *(distant)*
  Lysander!

LYSANDER
  When I come where he calls, then he is gone,
  And I am fallen in dark uneven way,
  And here will rest me. Come, thou gentle day.   [24, 9]

Lies down.

For if but once thou show me thy grey light
  I'll find Demetrius, and revenge this spite.

He sleeps.

Enter Puck.   [5]

PUCK
Ho, ho, ho, coward, why com'st thou not?

DEMETRIUS *(distant)*
Abide me if thou darest. Where are thou now?

PUCK
Come hither, I am here.

Enter Demetrius.

DEMETRIUS
Nay then, thou mock'st me; thou shalt buy this dear,
If ever I thy face by daylight see.
Now go thy way; faintness constraineth me   [24, 9]
To measure out my length on this cold bed.
By day's approach look to be visited.

Lies down and sleeps.

Enter Puck, followed by Helena.   [5]

HELENA
O weary night, O long and tedious night,   [24, 9]
Abate thy hours, shine comforts from the East,
And sleep that sometimes shuts up sorrow's eye
Steal me awhile from mine own company.

Sleeps.

PUCK
Yet but three? Come one more,   [5]
Two of both kinds makes up four.
Here she comes, curst and sad,

(Enter Hermia.)

Cupid is a knavish lad
Thus to make poor females mad.

HERMIA
Never so weary, never so in woe,
Bedabbled with the dew, and torn with briers,

I can no further crawl, no further go,   [24, 9]
My legs can keep no pace with my desires.
Here will I rest me till the break of day.
Heaven shield Lysander, if they mean a fray.

She sleeps.

Enter Fairies, very stealthily.

FAIRIES
On the ground, sleep sound: [47]
He'll apply to your eye,
Gentle lover, remedy.
When thou wak'st, thou tak'st
True delight in the sight
Of thy former lady's eye:
And the country proverb known,
In your waking shall be shown:
Jack shall have Jill,
Nought shall go ill,
The man shall have his mare again,
And all shall be well.

Exeunt Fairies.

Puck squeezes juice on Lysander's eyes and goes out.

(Curtain)

ACT THREE

[48]

The Wood, early next morning

Puck and Oberon appear.

OBERON *(observing Tytania)*
　My gentle Robin; see'st thou this sweet sight?
　Her dotage now I do begin to pity.
　And now I have the boy, I will undo
　This hateful imperfection of her eyes.
　Be as thou wast wont to be; [49]
　See as thou wast wont to see.
　Dian's bud, o'er Cupid's flower,
　Hath such force and blessed power.
　Now my Tytania wake you my sweet queen. [48]

Tytania wakes.

TYTANIA
　My Oberon, what visions I have seen! [50]
　Methought I was enamour'd of an ass.

OBERON
　There lies your love.

TYTANIA
　How came these things to pass?
　Oh, how mine eyes do loathe his visage now!

OBERON
　Silence awhile. Robin take off this head:
　Tytania, music call, and strike more dead
　Than common sleep, of all these five the sense.

TYTANIA
Music, ho music, such as charmeth sleep.

OBERON
Sound music; come my Queen, take hands with me
And rock the ground whereon these sleepers be.   [51]

They dance.

Now thou and I are new in amity
And will this very midnight, solemnly
Dance in Duke Theseus' house triumphantly,
And bless it to all fair prosperity.
There shall the pairs of faithful lovers be
Wedded, with Theseus, all in jollity.

PUCK
Fairy King attend, and mark,
I do hear the morning lark.

Exit Puck. Oberon and Tytania disappear, still dancing.

Distant horns.   [48, 52]

DEMETRIUS *(waking)*
Helena!

LYSANDER *(waking)*
Hermia!

HELENA *(waking)*
Demetrius!

HERMIA *(waking)*
Lysander!

LYSANDER
Are you sure that we are awake? It seems to me
That we yet sleep, we dream.

HERMIA
Methinks I see these things with parted eye,
When everything seems double.

DEMETRIUS
These things seem small and undistinguishable,
Like far-off mountains turned into clouds.

HELENA
So methinks;

ALL FOUR LOVERS

And I have found ⎡ Demetrius
⎢ Lysander
⎢ Sweet Hermia   like a jewel,
⎣ Fair Helen
Mine own, and not mine own.   [53]
Why then we are awake; let's go,
And by the way let us recount our dreams.   [10]

Exeunt lovers.

Bottom awakes.

BOTTOM
When my cue comes, call me, and I will answer. My next is,
Most fair Pyramus. Heigh-ho. Peter Quince? Flute the bellows-
mender? Snout the tinker? Starveling? [28] God's my life! Stolen
hence and left me asleep; I have had a dream, past the wit of man
to say what dream it was. [54] Methought I was, there is no man
can tell what. Methought I was, and methought I had. But man
is but an ass, if he will offer to say what methought I had. The
eye of man hath not heard, the ear of man hath not seen, man's
hand is not able to taste, his tongue to conceive, nor his heart to
report, what my dream was. [33, 16] I will get Peter Quince the
carpenter to write a ballad of this dream, and it shall be called
Bottom's Dream because it hath no bottom; [55] and I will sing
it in the latter end of the play, before the Duke. Peradventure, to
make it the more gracious, I shall sing it at her death.

Exit.

Enter Quince, Flute, Snout and Starveling.

QUINCE
Have you sent to Bottom's house? Is he come home yet?   [56]

STARVELING
He cannot be heard of. Out of doubt he is transported.

FLUTE
If he come not, then the play is marr'd. It goes not forward, doth it?

STARVELING
It is not possible: you have not a man in all Athens, able to discharge Pyramus but he.

SNOUT
No, he hath simply the best wit of any handicraft man in Athens.

QUINCE
Yea, and the best person too.

Enter Snug the joiner.

SNUG
Masters, the Duke is coming from the Temple. If our sport had gone forward, we had all been made men.

FLUTE
O sweet bully Bottom: thus hath he lost sixpence a day, during his life. And the Duke had not given him sixpence a day for playing Pyramus, I'll be hang'd. He would have deserved it. Sixpence a day in Pyramus, or nothing.

THE OTHERS
He could not have scaped it. Sixpence a day.

BOTTOM *(off)*
Where are these lads? Where are these hearts?

Enter Bottom.

ALL
Bottom, O most courageous day!

BOTTOM

Masters, I am to discourse wonders; but ask me not what.

ALL

Let us hear, sweet Bottom.

BOTTOM

Not a word of me: all that I will tell you, is that the Duke hath
dined and our play is preferred.   [16]

ALL *(except Bottom)*

Our play is preferred. Most dear actors get your apparel together;
good strings to your beards, new ribbons to your pumps; and
ev'ry man look o'er his part. Let Thisby have clean linen; let not
the Lion pare his nails; eat no onions, eat no garlic, that all may
say: It is a sweet Comedy.

BOTTOM

No more words: to the Palace, away, go, away.

Exeunt.

TRANSFORMATION SCENE TO THESEUS' PALACE   [57, 58]

Enter Theseus and Hippolyta with their court.

THESEUS

Now fair Hippolyta, our nuptial hour   [58]
Draws on apace: this happy day brings in
Another moon: But oh, methinks, how slow
This old moon wanes; she lingers my desires
Like to a Step-dame, or a Dowager,
Long withering out a young man's revenue.

HIPPOLYTA

This day will quickly steep itself in night;
This night will quickly dream away the time:
And then the Moon like to a silver bow

131

Now bent in Heaven, shall behold the night
Of our solemnities.   [52]

THESEUS
    Hippolyta, I woo'd thee with my sword
    And won thy love, doing thee injuries:
    But I wed thee in another key,
    With pomp, with triumph, and with revelling.

Enter Lysander, Demetrius, Helena and Hermia.   [9]

They kneel.

ALL LOVERS
    Pardon my Lord.

THESEUS
    I pray you all stand up.
    I know you two were rival enemies.
    How came this gentle concord in the world?

LYSANDER
    My Lord, I shall reply amazedly;
    I went with Hermia thither. Our intent
    Was to be gone from Athens, where we might,
    Without the peril of the Athenian law…

DEMETRIUS
    My Lord, fair Helen told me of their stealth,
    And I in fury thither follow'd them;
    Fair Helena in fancy following me.
    But, my good Lord…

THESEUS
    Fair lovers,
    Of this discourse we more will hear anon.
    Hermia, I will o'erbear your father's will;
    For in the Temple, by and by with us,
    These couples shall eternally be knit.

with HIPPOLYTA

Joy gentle friends, joy and fresh days of love,
Accompany your hearts.

The lovers embrace.

THESEUS
Come now, what masques, what dances shall we have,
Between our after-supper, and bed-time?

Enter Quince with play bill. He hands it to Hippolyta and bows.

HIPPOLYTA *(reading)*
A tedious brief scene of young Pyramus,
And his love Thisby; very tragical mirth.

LYSANDER
Merry and tragical? tedious and brief?

DEMETRIUS
That is, hot ice, and wondrous strange snow.

THESEUS
What are they that do play it?

HIPPOLYTA
Hard-handed men, that work in Athens here,
Which never labour'd in their minds till now;

THESEUS
I will hear that play.

Exit Quince.

For never any thing can be amiss,
When simpleness and duty tender it.
Take your places, Ladies.

Enter the Prologue (all rustics).   [59]

Theseus, Hippolyta and the Court take their places.

ALL RUSTICS
If we offend, it is with our good will.   [60]
That you should think, we come not to offend,

133

But with good will. To show our simple skill,
That is the true beginning of our end.
Consider then, we come but in despite.
We do not come, as minding to content you,
Our true intent is. All for your delight, [61]
We are not here. That you should here repent you,
The actors are at hand: and by their show,
You shall know all, that you are like to know.

THESEUS
These fellows do not stand upon points.

LYSANDER
They have rid their Prologue, like a rough colt:
They know not the stop.

HERMIA
It is not enough to speak but to speak true.

DEMETRIUS
Indeed they have played on their Prologue, like a child on a recorder,

HELENA
A sound but not in government.

HIPPOLYTA
Their speech was like a tangled chain; nothing impaired, but all disordered.

THESEUS
Who is next?

PROLOGUE (Quince)
Gentles, perchance you wonder at this show, [62]
But wonder on, till truth makes all things plain.
This man is Pyramus, if you would know;
This beauteous Lady, Thisby is certain.
This man, with lime and rough-cast, doth present
Wall, that vile Wall, which did these lovers sunder:
This man, with lanthorn, dog, and bush of thorn,

Presenteth Moonshine.
This grisly beast is Lion hight by name.
For all the rest,
Let Lion, Moonshine, Wall and Lovers twain,
At large discourse, while here they do remain.

Exeunt all but Wall.

HELENA
I wonder if the Lion be to speak.

DEMETRIUS
No wonder, fair Lady: one Lion may, when many asses do.

WALL *(Snout)*
In this same Interlude, it doth befall,   [63]
That I, one Snout (by name) present a wall:
And such a wall, as I would have you think,
That had in it a crannied hole or chink:
And this the cranny is, right and sinister,
Through which the fearful Lovers are to whisper.

HERMIA
Would you desire lime and hair to sing better?

LYSANDER
It is the wittiest partition, that ever I heard discourse.

THESEUS
Pyramus draws near the Wall, silence.

Enter Pyramus.

PYRAMUS *(Bottom)*
O grim-look'd night, O night with hue so black,   [64]
O night, which ever art, when day is not:
O night, O night, alack, alack, alack,
I fear my Thisby's promise is forgot.
And thou O wall, O sweet, O lovely wall,   [65]
That stand'st between her father's ground and mine,
Thou wall, O wall, O sweet and lovely wall,
Show me thy chink, to blink through with mine eyne.

Thanks courteous wall. Jove shield thee well for this.
But what see I? No Thisby do I see.
O wicked wall, through whom I see no bliss,
Curs'd be thy stones for thus deceiving me.

THESEUS
The wall methinks being sensible, should curse again.

BOTTOM
No in truth sir, he should not. *Deceiving me* is Thisby's cue;
yonder she comes.

Enter Thisby. [66]

THISBY *(Flute)*
O wall, full often hast thou heard my moans, [67]
For parting my fair Pyramus, and me.
My cherry lips have often kiss'd thy stones:
Thy stones with lime and hair knit up in thee.

PYRAMUS
I see a voice; now will I to the chink,
To spy and I can hear my Thisby's face.
Thisby?

THISBY
My Love thou art, my Love I think. [68]

PYRAMUS
Think what thou wilt, I am thy Lover's grace.
O kiss me through the hole of the vile wall.

They kiss.

THISBY
I kiss the wall's hole, not your lips at all.

PYRAMUS
Wilt thou at Ninny's tomb meet me straightway?

THISBY
'Tide life, 'tide death, I come without delay.

Exeunt Pyramus and Thisby.

WALL
  Thus have I Wall, my part discharged so;
  And being done, thus Wall away doth go.

Exit.

HIPPOLYTA
  This is the silliest stuff that ever I heard.

THESEUS
  The best in this kind are but shadows, and the worst are no
  worse, if imagination amend them. Here come two noble beasts
  in, a man and a Lion.

Enter Lion and Moonshine.

LION *(Snug)*
  You Ladies, you (whose gentle hearts do fear   [69]
  The smallest monstrous mouse that creeps on floor)
  Should know that I, one Snug the joiner am
  A Lion fell, nor else no Lion's dam:

HERMIA
  A very gentle beast, and of a good conscience.

DEMETRIUS
  The very best at a beast that e'er I saw.

THESEUS
  But let us listen to the Moon.

MOONSHINE *(Starveling)*
  This lanthorn doth the horned Moon present: [70]

LYSANDER
  He should have worn the horns on his head.

MOONSHINE *(Starveling)*
  Myself the man i' th' Moon do seem to be.

THESEUS
The man should be put into the lanthorn. How is it else the man i' th' Moon?

MOONSHINE
This lanthorn doth the horn...

DEMETRIUS
He dares not come there for the candle.

THESEUS
Proceed Moon.

MOONSHINE
All I have to tell you is that this lanthorn is the Moon; I, the man i' th' Moon; this thorn-bush, my thorn-bush; and this dog, my dog.

HIPPOLYTA
I am weary of this Moon; would he would change.

ALL
But silence; here comes Thisby.

Enter Thisby.

THISBY
This is old Ninny's tomb. Where is my love?

LION
Oh.   [71]

The Lion roars. Thisby runs off, dropping mantle.

DEMETRIUS
Well roar'd Lion.

THESEUS
Well run Thisby.

LYSANDER
Well moused Lion.

HERMIA
   Well run Thisby.

HIPPOLYTA
   Well shone Moon.

HELENA
   Truly the Moon shines with a good grace.

Exit Lion.

Enter Pyramus.

PYRAMUS
   Sweet Moon, I thank thee for thy sunny beams,   [72]
   I thank thee Moon, for shining now so bright;
   But stay; O spite! but mark, poor Knight,
   What dreadful dole is here?
   Eyes do you see! how can it be!
   O dainty duck: O dear!
   Thy mantle good; what stain'd with blood!
   Approach, ye Furies fell: [73]
   O Fates! come, come: cut thread and thrum,
   Quail, crush, conclude, and quell.

HIPPOLYTA
   Beshrew my heart, but I pity the man.

PYRAMUS
   O wherefore Nature, didst thou Lions frame?
   Since Lion vile hath here deflower'd my dear:
   Which is: no, no, which was the fairest Dame.
   Come tears, confound: out sword, and wound
   The pap of Pyramus:
   Thus die I, thus, thus, thus.
   Now am I dead, now am I fled, my soul is in the sky,
   Tongue lose thy light, Moon take thy flight.

Exit Moonshine.

   Now die, die, die, die, die.

Dies.

DEMETRIUS
With the help of a surgeon, he might yet recover, and prove an ass.

Enter Thisby.

THESEUS
Here Thisby comes, and her passion ends the play.

HIPPOLYTA
I hope she will be brief.

THISBY
Asleep my Love? What, dead my dove? [74]
O Pyramus arise:
Speak, speak. Quite dumb? Dead, dead? A tomb [75]
Must cover thy sweet eyes.
These lily lips, this cherry nose, [76]
These yellow cowslip cheeks,
Are gone, are gone: Lovers make moan:
His eyes were green as leeks.
Tongue not a word: come trusty sword:
Come blade, my breast imbrue:
And farewell friends, thus Thisby ends;

She stabs herself.

Adieu, adieu, adieu.

THESEUS
Moonshine and Lion are left to bury the dead.

DEMETRIUS
Ay, and Wall too.

BOTTOM
No, I assure you, the wall is down that parted their fathers. Will it please you to see the Epilogue, or to hear a Bergomask dance?

Bottom (Pyramus) and Flute (Thisby) get up.

THESUS
No Epilogue, I pray; for your play needs no excuse.
But come, your Bergomask:

*The other rustics come in and arrange themselves for a Bergomask
dance.* [77] *Midnight sounds.* [78] *The dance stops, and the rustics
bow to the Duke and the others, and leave.*

THESEUS
The iron tongue of midnight hath told twelve.
Lovers to bed, 'tis almost fairy time.
I fear we shall out-sleep the coming morn,
As much as we this night have overwatch'd.
Sweet friends to bed.

ALL
Sweet friends to bed.

Exeunt.

Enter Fairies.

SOLO FAIRIES
Now the hungry lion roars,   [79]
And the wolf behowls the Moon:
Whilst the heavy ploughman snores,
All with weary task fordone.
Now the wasted brands do glow,
Whilst the screech-owl, screeching loud,
Puts the wretch that lies in woe,
In remembrance of a shroud.
Now it is the time of night,
That graves, all gaping wide,
Every one lets forth his sprite,
In the church-way paths to glide.
And we Fairies, that do run,
By the triple Hecate's team,
From the presence of the Sun,
Following darkness like a dream,
Now are frolic; not a mouse
Shall disturb this hallow'd house.

Enter Puck with broom – he chases the Fairies.   [5]

PUCK
    I am sent with broom before,
    To sweep the dust behind the door.

Enter the King and Queen of the Fairies with all their train.

OBERON
    Through the house give glimmering light,   [6]
    Every elf and fairy sprite,
    Sing this ditty after me,
    Sing and dance it trippingly.

TYTANIA
    First rehearse your song by rote,
    To each word a warbling note.

BOTH
    Hand in hand, with fairy grace,
    Will we sing and bless this place.

OBERON, TYTANIA and FAIRIES
    Now until the break of day,   [80]
    Through this house each Fairy stray.
    To the best bride-bed will we,
    Which by us shall blessed be:
    And the issue there create,
    Ever shall be fortunate:
    So shall all the couples three,
    Ever true and loving be.
    With this field-dew consecrate,
    Every Fairy take his gait,
    And each several chamber bless,
    Through this Palace with sweet peace,
    Ever shall in safety rest,
    And the owner of it blest.

OBERON
    Trip away, make no stay;
    Meet me all by break of day.

Exeunt all but Puck.

PUCK
    If we shadows have offended,   [5]
    Think but this (and all is mended)
    That you have but slumber'd here,
    While these visions did appear.
    Gentles, do not reprehend.
    If you pardon, we will mend.
    Else the Puck a liar call.
    So good night unto you all.
    Give me your hands, if we be friends,
    And Robin shall restore amends.

(Quick curtain)

Discography

YEAR	CAST	CONDUCTOR/ORCHESTRA	LABEL
	OBERON		
	TYTANIA		
	PUCK		
	THESEUS		
	HIPPOLYTA		
	LYSANDER		
	DEMETRIUS		
	HERMIA		
	HELENA		
	BOTTOM		
1966	Alfred Deller Elizabeth Harwood Stephen Terry John Shirley-Quirk Helen Watts Peter Pears Thomas Hemsley Josephine Veasey Heather Harper Owen Brannigan	Benjamin Britten London Symphony Orchestra	Decca
1993	James Bowman Lillian Watson Dexter Fletcher Norman Bailey Penelope Walker John Graham-Hall Henry Herford Della Jones Jill Gomez Donald Maxwell	Richard Hickox City of London Sinfonia	Virgin Classics

1996	Brian Asawa	Colin Davis	Philips
	Sylvia McNair	London Symphony Orchestra	
	Carl Ferguson		
	Brian Bannatyne-Scott		
	Hilary Summers		
	John Mark Ainsley		
	Paul Whelan		
	Ruby Philogene		
	Janice Watson		
	Robert Lloyd		

A Midsummer Night's Dream on DVD

YEAR	CAST	CONDUCTOR	DIRECTOR/COMPANY
	OBERON TYTANIA PUCK THESEUS HIPPOLYTA LYSANDER DEMETRIUS HERMIA HELENA BOTTOM		
1981	James Bowman Ileana Cotrubas Damien Nash Lieuwe Visser Claire Powell Ryland Davies Dale Duesing Cynthia Buchan Felicity Lott Curt Appelgren	Bernard Haitink	Peter Hall Glyndebourne Festival
2005	David Daniels Ofelia Sala Emil Wolk Ned Barth Jean Rigby Gordon Gietz William Dazeley Deanne Meek Brigitte Hahn Peter Rose	Harry Bicket	Robert Carsen Gran Teatre del Liceu, Barcelona

Select Bibliography

Blyth, Alan (ed.), *Remembering Britten* (London: Hutchinson, 1981)

Brett, Philip, *Music and Sexuality in Britten* (Berkeley: University of California Press, 2006)

Carpenter, Humphrey, *Benjamin Britten: a Biography* (London: Faber and Faber, 1992)

Cooke, Mervyn (ed.), *The Cambridge Companion to Benjamin Britten* (Cambridge: Cambridge University Press, 1999)

Evans, Peter, *The Music of Benjamin Britten* (London: J. M. Dent, rev. edn., 1989)

Godsalve, William H.L., *Britten's 'A Midsummer Night's Dream': Making an Opera from Shakespeare's Comedy* (London and Toronto: Associated University Presses, 1995)

Herbert, David, *The Operas of Benjamin Britten* (London: Hamish Hamilton, 1979)

Kennedy, Michael, *Britten* (London: J.M. Dent, rev. edn., 1993)

Kildea, Paul (ed.), *Britten on Music* (Oxford, Oxford University Press 2003)

Mitchell, Donald and John Evans, *Pictures from a Life: Benjamin Britten, 1913–1976* (London: Faber and Faber, 1978)

Oliver, Michael, *Benjamin Britten* (London: Phaidon Press, 1996)

Palmer, Christopher (ed.), *The Britten Companion* (London: Faber and Faber, 1984)

Reed, Philip and Cooke Mervyn (eds), *Letters from a Life: The Selected Letters of Benjamin Britten 1913–1976*, vol. 5 (Woodbridge: The Boydell Press, 2010)

Seymour, Claire, *The Operas of Benjamin Britten: Expression and Evasion* (Woodbridge: The Boydell Press, 2004)

Shakespeare, William, *A Midsummer Night's Dream* edited by G. B. Harrison (Harmondsworth: Penguin, 1953). [This was the edition used by Britten and Pears to devise their libretto.]

Walker, Lucy (ed.), *Benjamin Britten: New Perspectives on his Life and Work* (Woodbridge: The Boydell Press, 2009)

White, Eric Walter, *Benjamin Britten, His Life and Operas*, rev. second edn., edited by John Evans (London: Faber and Faber, 1983)

Britten Websites

The website of the Britten–Pears Foundation in Aldeburgh is extremely comprehensive and well maintained. It contains detailed information about Britten's life and works, as well as links that allow further research. Britten's publishers, Boosey and Hawkes, Chester Novello and Faber Music, also provide full information about his published works:

www.brittenpears.org
www.boosey.com
www.chesternovello.com
www.fabermusic.com

Note on the Contributors

Andrew Plant received his doctorate from the University of Birmingham and was based at the Britten–Pears Foundation for many years, from where he forged a dual career as a musicologist and practical musician. As a pianist he has enjoyed a particularly fruitful recital partnership with James Bowman, recording for Signum Classics and NMC.

Philip Reed is Head of Publications at ENO. His many writings on Britten include five volumes of the composer's selected letters (co-edited with Donald Mitchell and Mervyn Cooke), an edition of Peter Pears's travel diaries, and contributions to studies of *Billy Budd*, *Gloriana*, *Peter Grimes* and *War Requiem*. His and Mervyn Cooke's sixth and final volume of Britten's correspondence is due for publication by the time of the composer's centenary in 2013.

David Nice is a writer, lecturer and broadcaster with a special interest in Russian music. His books include the first volume of a Prokofiev biography for Yale University Press and short studies of Elgar, Richard Strauss, Stravinsky, Tchaikovsky and the history of opera. He was a Hesse Student at Aldeburgh in 1983 and 1984.

Philip Brett was a musicologist, musician and conductor. In addition to his work on William Byrd, his pioneering studies on gay and lesbian sexuality in music led to the eventual integration of these disciplines into mainstream academic discourse. His publications include *Music and Sexuality in Britten*. He died in 2002.

Acknowledgements

We would like to thank John Allison of *Opera* magazine, Dr Nicholas Clark of the Britten–Pears Foundation, James Bowman and Charles Johnston for their assistance and advice in the preparation of this guide. We are also extremely grateful to Andy Chan of Boosey and Hawkes Ltd.